Able, Gifted and Ta

The SEN series

Able, Gifted and Talented

Janet Bates and Sarah Munday

continuum

Continuum International Publishing Group
The Tower Building
11 York Road
London SE1 7NX

15 East 26th Street
New York
NY 10010

www.continuumbooks.com

British Library Cataloguing-in-Publication Data
A catalogue record for this book is available from the British Library.

ISBN 08264–7837–9 (paperback)

Typeset by BookEns Ltd, Royston, Herts.
Printed and bound in Great Britain by
MPG Books Ltd, Bodmin, Cornwall

1005077665

Contents

Acknowledgements

Many thanks are due to Judith Weaver, Nicola Young and Su Chamberlain, for their collaboration in the Best Practice Research Project that helped to shape a number of the views that are expressed in this book.

1

Providing for Able, Gifted and Talented Pupils: Identification and Strategies for Schools

Over the last few years, there has developed a growing recognition of the importance of meeting the educational needs of our more able, gifted and talented children within our educational system. Historically, there has tended to be a strongly held belief among many educators that a child of above average abilities will naturally achieve his or her potential, without the need for specific intervention or challenging strategies. However, as schools have become accustomed to using information derived from data as part of whole-school and departmental planning processes, it has become clear it may often be the more able children in our schools who fail to make the progress that we really should expect them to make: they fail to reach their potential.

This should not be a surprise to us – history is littered with figures whose potential was not fully recognized at school, yet who have nevertheless managed to achieve success in their own right. Winston Churchill, John Lennon and Stephen Fry are three very famous cases in point; in fact, Stephen Fry's last English report from Uppingham School in

1972 simply reads 'Bottom, rightly'. Fry, like many others, seems to have achieved his success in spite of his lack of motivation at school. What must concern us as teachers is the number of able, gifted and talented children whose abilities are never recognized; who therefore are never given the opportunities to 'fly', and who sink without a trace. These are the children who should become the leaders for our future; scientists, educationalists, and economic and cultural leaders who could play a significant role in transforming the world of the twenty-first century. The world of the future is perhaps more uncertain than it has ever been; our able, gifted and talented pupils need to be adaptable, creative and quick thinking if they are to make their mark on that world.

There is still, to some extent, an uncomfortable feeling that to identify and specifically provide for able, gifted and talented pupils is perhaps a form of elitism; that we may be accused of providing unfair opportunities for these pupils who will probably succeed 'anyway'. Yet at the same time we clearly see the need to intervene with less able pupils, or pupils with specific learning difficulties, in order to ensure that they have the best possible opportunities in life. Our able, gifted and talented pupils have the same rights to a curriculum that caters for their individual needs, and which allows them to develop their strengths in an ethos where diversity is both recognized and celebrated. Schools can – and should – make a difference in pupils' lives; we as teachers should be prepared, in the words of Deborah Eyre, to become experts in both 'spotting' and 'nurturing' the gifts and talents in our classrooms.

Providing for Able, Gifted and Talented Pupils

All pupils, including the gifted and talented, develop and flourish in schools with deliberate strategies for raising self-esteem and where all forms of success are overtly valued. Schools that have specifically focused on the needs of the more able within their classrooms have realized that they have also made a real difference, in terms of self-esteem and achievement, with pupils of all abilities. In taking away the 'artificial ceilings' on achievement, we allow all pupils the opportunities to show what they **can** do – rather than what they can't do. The raising of teachers' expectations of pupils' potential clearly has an impact on the attitudes and achievement of the pupils they teach. Therefore, in order to be truly inclusive, schools should consider:

- raising awareness among all school staff, governors and parents of the needs of able, gifted and talented pupils;

- developing procedures for the identification of able, gifted and talented pupils across the curriculum;

- tracking and monitoring the progress of identified pupils;

- developing clear, transparent and sharing strategies for challenging and supporting these pupils within and outside the curriculum;

- accessing all available sources of support for able, gifted and talented pupils.

What do we mean by 'gifted and talented' pupils?

Education Department guidelines state that 'gifted and talented pupils are those pupils who achieve, or have the ability to achieve, at a level significantly in advance of the average for their year group' (DfEE 1999, Excellence in Cities). In addition, gifted children are defined as those who exhibit high ability across one or more academic subject areas; and talented children are those who excel in a specific area: either socially – in terms of leadership – or in sport, the performing arts or design and technology. Gifted and talented children are those who exhibit all round ability, across a wide variety of subjects.

Key questions that schools should therefore consider are:

♦ How do we ensure that we recognize the potential in a child who is not yet fully demonstrating his or her giftedness or talent?

♦ How do we create the optimum opportunities for all children to demonstrate their potential?

'Education is not about what children can do, but about what they might achieve with the guidance of their teachers' (Challenging Able Pupils: Guidelines for Secondary Schools). In identifying their able, gifted and talented cohort, schools also need to be aware that certain factors, including uneven rates of intellectual development, intervention from within and outside the school, and the effects of the home or school environment, can radically affect the achievement of an individual. Teachers should be constantly vigilant for signs of underachievement with these pupils and be ready to take steps to intervene.

No school can say it has no gifted or talented pupils. An obvious consequence is that the composition of the gifted and talented population is likely to vary ... Pupils regarded as gifted and talented in one school may not be considered so in another school whose intake of pupils is dissimilar.

('Providing for Gifted and Talented Pupils', Ofsted 2001)

Schools within the Excellence in Cities initiative are in receipt of DfES funding for gifted and talented pupils within their LEAs, and are expected to identify between 5 per cent and 10 per cent of each year group. It is important to note that the expectation is that this percentage of pupils will be identified within the context of each school; a tiny primary school, a secondary modern school and a grammar school should all identify up to 10 per cent of their particular cohort in each year group. However, many schools have found in practice that the list of pupils can be as much as 30 per cent of each year group, when those children with specific talents are taken into account. In addition, the list should be regularly reviewed and will probably change from year to year, in recognition of the fact that all children are unique. Once identified, the majority of pupils will continue to develop and to demonstrate high ability; others may find that they reach a plateau, or may in fact not have had that higher potential. Therefore the issue of identification does need a fair and transparent policy, and very sensitive handling. A significant decision that schools should make is: what proportion of the pupils on the identified list should already be achieving highly; and what proportion of pupils on the list should consist of those who may have the potential to achieve highly in the future.

Typical characteristics of able, gifted and talented pupils

Gifted and talented pupils will often have high IQ; demonstrated in the NFER tests, the CATs tests, MidYIS, SATs, YELLIS and ALIS and other Intelligence Scale tests. However, parents and teachers should not place total reliance on these standardized tests, as there are other typical attributes of very able children.

Gifted and talented pupils will usually demonstrate a combination of some of the following characteristics:

◆ an early ability to speak in sentences and to sustain a conversation with an adult;

◆ a wide vocabulary and excellent reading ability;

◆ an inveterate curiosity and a questioning attitude;

◆ an ability for sustained concentration particularly when the subject really interests them;

◆ demonstrating a preference for complex thought;

◆ able to work with abstract thought, often using higher level thinking skills (see Chapter 3);

◆ showing a preference for socializing with older pupils, or with adults – they sometimes have difficulty making friends within their own peer group;

- an excellent memory; able to retain and then transfer information;

- a sense of humour that may be considered 'quirky' or 'odd' by other pupils and teachers;

- a delight in language play, such as puns;

- challenging behaviour, particularly when bored or frustrated;

- an ability to make links between abstract concepts;

- a dislike of perceived 'failure', and sometimes an inability to accept being 'wrong';

- a vivid imagination;

- impatience with schoolwork which they feel lacks real purpose;

- possessing wide general knowledge;

- preferring individual work rather than collaborating in a group – a tendency to be impatient with others who do not think as quickly;

- leadership skills.

We need to remember that, however bright a child may be, he or she is first and foremost a child; and must be given the time and space needed to develop as a whole person. Teachers sometimes feel a little uneasy about teaching a child whose intellectual capacity is possibly well above their own. But children of all ages need to learn socially and emotionally as well as academically, and should be given opportunities to develop the invaluable skills of collaborative learning, of leadership and of negotiation. Above all, able, gifted and talented children must learn that there is often no 'right ' or 'wrong' answer; and that learning from mistakes is an essential part of the total learning experience. This important issue will be discussed further in Chapter 3.

Identification issues for teachers and parents

Much has been written about the identification of able, gifted and talented children; yet it undoubtedly remains the most problematic aspect of the gifted and talented initiative. This is because, as indicated earlier, children develop at different rates according to their home and school influences, and their potential for achievement may well remain undiscovered and untapped until well into their teenage years. Teachers and parents therefore need to be aware of the indicators of giftedness or talent, and use a range of methods for identifying potential that is 'in advance' of a child's age or year group.

Standardized tests

There are a range of quantitative tests that the majority of schools routinely administer that can be used to help to identify able, gifted and talented pupils. These include:

♦ Foundation Stage assessments

♦ Key Stage 1 assessments

- Key Stage 2 SAT tests in English, Maths and Science
- NFER tests
- Reading tests
- Cognitive Ability Tests
- MidYIS
- World Class Tests in Number and Problem Solving
- Key Stage 3 SAT tests
- YELLIS
- GCSE examinations
- ALIS and ALPS
- AS level examinations
- A level examinations

Although these standardized tests are extremely useful in terms of raw data, it is very important that they are not used in isolation. Staff, parents, pupils and carers should all have a part to play in identifying potential; and the procedures must be rigorous and fair.

Other identification strategies

Identification strategies may also include:

- identification by teaching staff and teaching assistants; using class work, coursework, test and assessment results, observation and, most importantly, their own professional judgements;

- information received from previous teachers or schools; from external agencies and organizations such as nurseries, playgroups, sports clubs or youth organizations and peripatetic services;

- information from parents and carers;

- information from the pupils themselves, and from their peers;

- the involvement of LEA support, such as education psychologists.

Many schools have found it helpful to create their own forms for nominating pupils and for gathering information about pupils who may be considered able, gifted or talented. This ensures that information from a range of sources is recorded and can be transferred to the schools' central data systems. In addition, schools may find it useful to have a separate form for use with parents, particularly at points of transition from one key stage to another (See Appendix 2).

Good communication within schools, and systems that facilitate the rapid transfer of information, are essential tools in recognizing and acknowledging potential. Schools should consider how efficiently they circulate information about pupils; how they enable all staff to gain a holistic picture of the children they teach; and how that information is used by individual teachers in order to inform their planning. The transition of pupils from year to year and from Key Stage to Key Stage is crucial in the transfer of both qualitative and quantitative information, and needs careful planning. In secondary schools in particular, it is possible to have a very narrow view of a child who may not be achieving particularly well in 'your' subject; yet that view may well be challenged if a teacher becomes aware that the same child is achieving very differently in one, or even a number of other subject areas. The creation of an ethos in which there is a constant sharing of information, celebrations and concerns about pupils across all subject areas and staff, is essential if a school is to progress along the path of personalized learning for all children. Strategies that schools may find helpful are listed below.

◆ Observation of specific pupils in a particular subject area or across a range of subject areas. These can be undertaken by Teaching Assistants and teachers, and should have agreed areas of focus that may include: interaction with others in the class, and with the teacher; responses to questions; ability to ask questions; levels of concentration and/or frustration; and a comparison of written and oral abilities.

◆ Individual interviews with pupils in order to ascertain their views about learning, about themselves and their progress in school.

◆ Questionnaires that enable pupils to identify their own perceptions of their strengths and weaknesses in learning generally, and in specific subject areas. These can also allow pupils the opportunity to reflect on interests and to celebrate successes outside the school.

◆ Subject-related or skills-related questionnaires that allow pupils the opportunity to nominate those among their peer group that they consider to have particular strengths.

◆ Learning logs: these may be kept by pupils as 'target books' in which they record their successes and their achievement goals.

Identifying the able underachievers

This is arguably one of the most important areas of provision for the able, gifted and talented in our classrooms. We have already made the point that we as teachers should be on the lookout for ability and talent within our classrooms, and therefore aware of the indicators of latent ability and talent. It can be very easy for a moderately able and hardworking child, who strives to please and is anxious to succeed, to be mistakenly identified as a child whose abilities are well above the average. At the same time, the real and potential abilities of a child who may be a disruptive influence in the classroom, who dislikes conventional writing tasks and tends to finish work with the least amount of effort, can be overlooked within the day-to-day pressures of the classroom situation.

Nevertheless, the sooner a child who is underachieving is recognized, the more opportunities there may be to intervene in order to motivate and stimulate in that child a desire to learn and to succeed. It is surely one of a school's most important functions to identify, to analyse and to take steps to overcome individual pupils' barriers to learning. A checklist giving the typical signs of potential underachievement can be helpful to teachers; however the context of the child's home and the school, and any other available information, should also be taken into account.

Typical characteristics of able and potentially disaffected underachievers

Able underachievers may well show a combination of the following characteristics:

◆ orally good, demonstrating quick thinking, the ability to build on other people's ideas and to apply learning in different situations;

◆ able to argue and justify with ease;

◆ poor written work; unfinished, untidy, completing the minimum to get by;

◆ may seem bored, lethargic and uninterested and anxious to finish the school day;

◆ may be restless and inattentive;

◆ able to manipulate other people and situations;

◆ able to ask searching and perhaps provocative and challenging questions;

◆ may find it easier to form relationships with older pupils and with adults, than with his/her own peer group;

◆ needs to know the reasons behind classroom activities – the 'what's in it for me' factor;

◆ may be disorganized both in terms of the practicalities of equipment etc, and also in terms of time management;

- able to escape into a private world, therefore may sit and do nothing for long periods both within and outside lessons;

- may be unpopular with peers because of an awareness of other people's weaknesses and a readiness to comment openly about them;

- may be quiet and withdrawn because he/she is unwilling to show ability for fear of peer pressure and/or bullying;

- can become easily frustrated, particularly when perceiving others in the class or group as too slow in intellectual terms; there may be a tendency to bad temper and mood swings.

Able underachievers need direct support and intervention; emotionally, socially and through motivation and challenge in the classroom. These areas will be explored in greater depth in Chapters 2 and 3.

Identification and withdrawal from the mainstream curriculum

Schools that have taken steps towards identifying and therefore specifically providing for their able, gifted and talented pupils have tried a range of strategies. Some have, to some extent, taken on the American and Australian models of withdrawing these pupils from mainstream teaching for a proportion of their time in school, in order to allow them to pursue a separate programme.

The advantages of this strategy are clear:

◆ able children are given structured opportunities to interact and learn together;

◆ a specific programme of activities can be created, at an appropriate level of challenge;

◆ schools can clearly show that they are aware of the needs of this group of pupils and that they have put intervention programmes in place.

However, there can be drawbacks, and schools need to be aware of the issues that arise – from the point of view of the pupils themselves. These issues are raised in the section on listening to able, gifted and talented pupils at the end of Chapter 3.

Key Messages from Chapter 1

◆ All pupils have a right to a broad and balanced curriculum that takes account of their individual needs and allows them the opportunities to reach their potential.

◆ Focusing on the needs of able, gifted and talented pupils in the classroom often has the effect of raising teachers' expectations of all pupils, and consequently raising the achievement of all pupils.

◆ Teachers and schools need to remove artificial ceilings to learning so all pupils are given opportunities to show what they can do and demonstrate their potential.

◆ Able, gifted and talented pupils should be

identified within the context of their school, not within a national context.

♦ Schools should use a range of strategies to identify able, gifted and talented pupils, and ensure that the information is circulated among, and discussed with, all members of staff and with the parents of identified pupils.

♦ Able, gifted and talented children need to be allowed every opportunity to develop socially and emotionally, as well as academically.

♦ Schools should take action to overcome individual pupils' barriers to learning; therefore teachers need to be aware of the indicators of potential underachievement in able, gifted and talented pupils, and take steps to intervene.

2

Developing a Whole-school Policy

If there is to be a consistent approach to teaching gifted and talented pupils in school, a whole-school policy of which all staff are aware of is vital. The aim should be to produce a holistic approach which is coherent:

◆ across subject areas;

◆ across different year groups;

◆ across different phases;

◆ for each gifted and talented pupil.

Teachers will be able to look to the policy for guidance and advice. The policy should raise the profile of the able, gifted and talented in the school as a whole and also provide a point of reference for staff. If the school is to make effective provision for able pupils the policy should form the foundation for this and should enhance the chances of success.

There are a variety of models for policies on which you may choose to base your own gifted and talented policy. Your LEA may have model policies on which you can draw, and other local schools can be a valuable source of material on which you can base a policy of your own. Appendix 1 provides an example of an able, gifted and talented policy that can be adapted for primary or secondary schools.

Able, Gifted and Talented

Ideally the policy should not be produced by the Gifted and Talented Coordinator alone. In order that staff have ownership of the policy and take an active interest in the issues involved, forming a working group to produce the policy is extremely useful. The staff involved in the working group should reflect a range of experience, responsibility and subject areas.

Below are some of the aspects which the policy should cover:

- the rationale for the policy;

- the aims and objectives, including an overview of how the school is approaching the teaching of able, gifted and talented pupils;

- a definition of gifted and talented; in particular a clear definition of the difference between these two terms, which are often confused;

- how able, gifted and talented pupils are identified not only in the school as a whole, but by individual teachers or departments;

- how the monitoring of pupils' progress will take place;

- which staff are responsible for the monitoring and the coordination of the able, gifted and talented programmes generally;

- how able, gifted and talented pupils will be challenged within class;

- how enrichment and extra-curricular activities may be used to support the able, gifted and talented pupils.

As with any policy it is important that it is updated on a regular basis to take account of changes within the school and any national developments. A policy needs to be a working document, not one that is left to gather dust on the shelf. Regularly revisiting the policy, and adapting it to suit the needs of those to whom it relates, will help to raise the profile of this issue with the wider teaching staff and give them a sense of ownership.

The next important stage is the monitoring and evaluation of the policy, and of the pupils themselves.

The role of the Gifted and Talented Coordinator

A number of schools appoint a member of staff to be the coordinator for able, gifted and talented pupils. It is important that someone on the staff fulfils this role, or is at least nominated to oversee the interests of this group of pupils and liaise with parents. It is generally accepted that schools have coordinators for a variety of curriculum areas and few question the need for a coordinator for Special Educational Needs; therefore an Able Gifted and Talented Coordinator should be seen as equally important. It is, however, better that the role of the Gifted and Talented Coordinator is kept separate from that of the Special Education Needs Coordinator if at all possible. Obviously, in small schools this may not be possible, but the demands on time for both roles are great, and therefore the combined role may well be too demanding for one person alone; particularly in a sizeable school. Also, the needs of the two groups of pupils involved are distinct and therefore better treated separately.

The main roles for the coordinator are: to co-ordinate the identification process; to develop the provision for able pupils both in the curriculum and through extra-curricular activities; and to liaise with parents and governors.

Identification of gifted and talented pupils

A number of systems may be employed by individual institutions in order to identify the able pupils in a school (see Chapter 1). The DfES defines gifted pupils as 'the most able 10–15 per cent of pupils'. Many institutions, for example The National Academy for Gifted and Talented Youth, focus on a narrrower group of the top 5 per cent of pupils. It is possible that if a school takes into account all of those with talents in one or more subject areas, the identified proportion of pupils may be nearer to 30–40 per cent. It is important that, whatever system is adopted for identification, this is open and clear to all involved. Individual teachers and departments should be involved in identifying pupils with particular strengths and provide feedback on these pupils to the coordinator.

Setting up a gifted and talented register

Once identified, it is important that a list of those pupils is produced. It is useful to provide as much information as possible regarding the achievements of these pupils, such as CAT and SAT scores, NFER tests, Key Stage SATs testing results, GCSE examination results and MidYIS/YELLIS scores. The register may also include information about outside interests and extra-curricular activities that each pupil undertakes. In addition, pupils who are talented in particular subject areas should also form a part of this list. The register should be circulated to all teaching staff, Teaching Assistants and departments in the school so that all staff have access to its contents.

It is also important to note that the register should not be seen as a 'finished product'; it needs to be updated on a regular basis to reflect the fact that pupils develop at different rates throughout their school careers. Highlighting high or underachieving pupils who appear on the register at staff/departmental meetings raises awareness among staff of who needs to be targeted as having the potential for high achievement.

There are issues associated with the transition between Key Stages, and in particular how information about able, gifted and talented pupils is communicated; for example, from primary to secondary schools. It is possible that a child who may have appeared on the register at his/her previous school may not be included at the new educational establishment. This issue needs to be handled sensitively by the Gifted and Talented Coordinator in open communication with the parents of the child. Any register should be set within the context of the school and must take account of the range of ability of pupils taught there. It should not be possible for any school to claim that it has no able, gifted or talented pupils.

Providing support for able, gifted and talented pupils in the school

This may take the form of mentoring specific pupils – particularly those who are able underachievers. Meeting with pupils to discuss their progress and to encourage and guide them in their development has proved one of the most effective methods of improving performance. Setting clear goals and challenges can be motivating for many able pupils. In their research on able underachievers Michael and Kathryn Anne Pomerantz stress the significance of providing a forum for able pupils to discuss openly what helps or hinders their progress. Indeed, those pupils who were interviewed valued staff who 'asked good questions', 'encouraged hard effort', 'set high expectations and standards', and 'rewarded good work and behaviour'. (Pomerantz and Pomerantz 2002). While this is undoubtedly a time consuming process, it is an extremely valuable process for both pupils and teaching staff. Sharing the responsibility for mentoring able pupils with other interested members of staff, or with members of the community, will help to ease the workload in this respect.

Reviewing the progress of able, gifted and talented pupils

It is important that the Gifted and Talented Coordinator has the overview of the development (or otherwise) of more able pupils within the school. It is useful if those involved in monitoring pupil progress, for example pastoral or Key Stage team leaders or Year Heads, provide feedback to the coordinator based on yearly reviews and the assessment, recording and reporting processes within the school. In this way the progress of individuals can be monitored closely. It is often interesting to interview individual pupils about their development, their feelings about the teaching that they receive, and their support generally. This, combined with observation of more able pupils in lessons, can be a useful method of monitoring teaching and learning outcomes for this cohort of pupils. It should be noted, however, that this aspect of monitoring can often be a sensitive area for staff and should be approached carefully; the aims and objectives of the exercise must be made transparent to all before such a process is undertaken.

Enable staff to access relevant information, materials and training relating to the teaching of able, gifted and talented pupils

The Gifted and Talented Coordinator needs to be able to support the staff of the school in understanding the needs of the more able pupils and assisting them in their continuing professional development in this respect. It is useful to set up a staff library to provide access to materials relevant to developing challenge in the classroom; such as differentiation, accelerated learning and thinking for learning. Some useful titles to include in your library will be found in the resources section of Chapter 5. Keeping a folder of relevant training courses and directing these to particular members of staff who may find these courses useful is also valuable. In addition, providing whole-school INSET or optional twilight INSET sessions on issues relating to the teaching of able, gifted and talented pupils will increase understanding of how to support these pupils in the school as a whole. While external speakers can often be inspirational and motivating, there are also a range of other people who can be involved in the training process. Support from consultancy staff in the LEA, Advanced Skills Teachers, and perhaps most importantly, drawing on the expertise of staff in your own and other local schools can be richly rewarding. It is often surprising just how much knowledge other staff have which can be shared with the wider school community.

Using established links with other schools to set up lesson observations by staff both in primary and secondary schools, and cross-phase observation, can be a very rewarding and informative process. Research suggests that teachers learn a great deal from considering how others teachers in their own and other subject areas/year groups approach the teaching of more able pupils. Setting up a group of staff with an interest in developing teaching and learning in the school, or in a cluster of schools, can also be a positive way of sharing the best practice among staff. It can provide a forum for staff to share ideas and concerns, pool resources, highlight particular pupils, and allow for staff to become involved in action research projects which are cross-curricular or cross-phase. Identifying literature which may be of interest to staff, or websites providing useful materials, and bringing these to the attention of those involved in provision, is often appreciated by staff.

Develop and organize enrichment and extra-curricular activities supported by various departments and staff within the school

In order that provision is coherent it is useful if the coordinator has an overview of the range of enrichment activities offered throughout the school. Mapping the opportunities offered to different categories of able, gifted and talented pupils in different year groups, and considering what additional opportunities might be offered in order to 'plug the gaps', is vitally important. Some activities may be subject related; such as involvement in orchestras or choirs, participating as a member of a school sports team, or taking part in a school production. Many extra-curricular activities can offer enrichment beyond the standard curriculum. Some good examples are highlighted later in this chapter. Involvement in enrichment days when pupils are withdrawn from lessons in order to take part in 'one-off' activities can also be useful to supplement the range of opportunities on offer. Promoting competitions and special events to highlight those in which the school can take part, is also part of this role. The Gifted and Talented Coordinator should not feel responsible for organizing all these activities, but should aim to encourage specialist staff, and those with particular interests in these areas, to be directly involved.

Liaison with outside agencies, across-school phases and with relevant groups in the local community

This is also a necessary part of the role of the Gifted and Talented Coordinator. Early identification of pupils on entry to the school is vital for real progress. Developing effective lines of communication with feeder schools is essential; and also provides the opportunity for cross-phase links, with older pupils working to support and mentor younger children. Using expertise outside the school to support teaching and learning, and looking to other agencies for additional input, is also a key aspect of the role.

Monitoring and evaluating the provision and support for the able, gifted and talented pupils

This is an integral part of the role; as well as making suggestions for training and development to the Leadership Team. It is important that the Gifted and Talented Coordinator has a voice on the Leadership Team, even if they themselves are not a part of it. Raising the profile of able, gifted and talented pupils should be seen as a vehicle for whole-school improvement and be an integral part of the School Improvement Plan.

Acting as a conduit for communication between pupils, staff and parents

All those involved in the progress of able, gifted and talented pupils need to be kept informed and updated regarding developments within the school and in the wider community. The coordinator is in the best position to provide this information and liaise between all the groups involved.

There are of course innumerable other areas which the Gifted and Talented Coordinator may assume as a part of the role. Some schools have gone down the route of drawing up Individual Education Plans (IEPs) for more able pupils. Producing materials which staff may draw on to support the more able in lessons is also a useful activity to undertake. If a budget is allocated for the provision for gifted and talented and/or enrichment activities, then the coordinator should be the one to manage this budget

Organizational issues

Every school or institution is different in the manner in which it organizes classes for teaching. No particular organizational method is better than any other but it is worth carefully considering how provision will be made for able, gifted and talented pupils within the classroom. It is important to recognize that no matter how good the extra-curricular and enrichment activities offered to more able pupils are, it is in the ordinary classroom that pupils receive the majority of their teaching and it is here that there must be sufficient challenge to extend the able pupil. Chapter 3 deals specifically with how challenge may be provided in the classroom, therefore this section considers the benefits of different types of classroom organization. The main options to consider are setting, streaming, mixed-ability grouping and fast tracking/withdrawal.

Setting

This strategy is used widely by schools in order to group pupils of similar abilities in a particular subject area. Setting should also allow for a student with a strength or talent in one particular subject area to have this recognized and rewarded through the individualized setting in that subject. The idea is that setting will allow lessons to be targeted at students of similar ability levels. Even within sets, however, there will be a range of ability, and therefore this method of organization does not remove the need for differentiation. It is not sufficient to place pupils in ability groups and then assume that the job is completed. Ideally there should be flexibility for pupils to move between sets based on achievement, and reviews of the pupils in sets should take place on a regular basis. It is also important that the Gifted and Talented Coordinator examines the set lists for different subjects, looking for anomalies in setting between similar subject areas and checking for underachievement against other data such as CATs scores. Primary schools often set pupils for Literacy and Numeracy, and may need to consider more flexibility in groupings, particularly in the light of DfES documentation on Excellence and Enjoyment.

Mixed-ability

Many schools feel that this is a more straightforward method of grouping pupils, although there is still a need to ensure that each group represents pupils from across the ability range. Clearly in such a group there is scope to develop more able pupils by allowing them to take leadership roles, to mentor less able pupils or to make small groups of able pupils responsible in part for elements of teaching. There needs, however, to be a strong emphasis on differentiation in groupings such as this, to ensure that those who are able are sufficiently stretched. The danger perhaps in this form of grouping in particular, is that able pupils will be allowed to 'get on with it', while those who find the work more difficult are supported. Thus the development of the able pupils may be hindered. There is a strong case for asking Teaching Assistants to work with more able pupils in the classroom, as well as the less able.

Streaming

This usually takes the form of grouping pupils by ability for all subjects or groups of subjects. While this does allow for some level of differentiation in grouping, there are issues with this method of organization. Some pupils are of roughly similar ability in all subject areas and some are gifted 'all rounders'. The ability of many pupils, however, differs from subject to subject; for example, the able mathematician may not be equally gifted in English. This method of organization is likely to fail to recognize the pupil who is talented in one particular subject area.

Fast tracking/withdrawal

Identifying pupils of high ability and placing them into a group to tackle their specific needs has advantages. The similar needs of the group may be more easily dealt with in this form of grouping and more challenging materials can be introduced. It is possible for such groups to take examinations early, i.e. to sit a GCSE in a subject a year or more in advance. The adoption of such an approach can, however, cause problems. Pupils in such a group are easily recognizable by other pupils and this may lead to peer targeting of these pupils. There is evidence to suggest that withdrawing the most able may not only disadvantage those of lower ability, who may not achieve as highly as a result, but also the able themselves. Certainly in terms of the comprehensive ethos, this approach is far from ideal. An alternative is that individual pupils can be selected for acceleration into a year above their chronological age. However, this must be considered very carefully as there are real social and emotional issues to be considered with regard to the maturity of the pupil, and the school leaving age.

Whichever method is selected, it is important that monitoring of able, gifted and talented pupils and their groupings takes place, in order to highlight any issues which are brought to light. In particular, underachievement and erratic groupings may only be picked up by a coordinator who has an overview of a pupil in all subject areas. It is also possible for the coordinator to make staff aware of more able pupils who are unusual in some way; for example, the pupil who has very high non-verbal reasoning scores in CATs testing but is dyslexic, and thus does not achieve highly in written testing. Procedures should be put in place to ensure that such pupils do not 'fall through the net'.

Enrichment and extra-curricular activities

While the focus of the provision in any school should primarily be on the teaching and learning within lessons themselves, enrichment activities can provide opportunities for leadership, and the development of skills and access to subject areas not generally offered in the course of the standard curriculum.

Many pupils undertake a wide range of activities outside of school and need minimal support in this respect. These should not be ignored as staff need to be aware of their pupils' achievements outside the school environment. Participation in activities, such as instrumental lessons, scouts and guides, The Duke of Edinburgh Award, and participating in sporting teams outside of school, can all be seen as part of the wider enrichment programme for individual pupils. Many pupils' involvement in such activities goes unrecorded and largely unnoticed by their school, and this is an important consideration. It is useful to develop some sort of system for collecting this sort of data on more able pupils. Some pupils may need more support than others in order to participate in activities out of school. Providing contact details and lists of associations and relevant groups can help to encourage some pupils to take part in such activities.

Within school, individual staff and departments often offer extra-curricular activities that help to challenge and extend pupils with specific talents or all-round ability. Drama and music clubs, sporting activities and school teams are often available for pupils to participate in. The school orchestra, wind band or choir can encourage talented musicians. There may also be the opportunity for able pupils to develop more unusual skills such as conducting small groups of musicians. Developing clubs and activities, such as a debating society or science club, producing a school newspaper, or chess and bridge clubs, allows pupils to develop a variety of new skills. Organizing trips as an enrichment activity can also help to develop specific talents and interests, whether these are to museums, the theatre or art galleries. Such activities benefit not only the more able but all pupils in the school community.

A number of universities offer enrichment open days where able pupils are encouraged to visit and take part in specific activities with specialist staff. Such days are also useful in encouraging able pupils to see that higher education is a stimulating experience in which they may wish to participate in future. Try to be aware of the opportunities offered by various universities – Oxford and Cambridge in particular are keen to encourage pupils from state schools to participate in these open days in order to highlight accessibility to all. Your local college or university may also be willing to offer support and expertise in areas that are of specific interest to pupils of all ages. Offering opportunities to take part in archaeological digs or engineering projects are just two examples of how staff and students from higher education institutes may be able to support enrichment for more able pupils.

Similarly, liaison between clusters of primary schools and local secondary schools, more especially schools with specialist status, may enable staff to tap into specific knowledge and expertise. In this way it may be possible to provide Masterclasses, Challenge Days, mentor able pupils, or set up email links where a teacher in secondary school provides support or comments on the work produced by more able primary school pupils.

Involvement in one-off or short-term activities can also form part of the enrichment programme offered by schools. These may be projects within school, such as Challenge Days involving clusters of primaries (see Chapter 5) where students are immersed in a particular subject for one day; or they may be linked to specific competitions or events such as Arts Festivals within school. Some areas to develop, or groups which may offer support to this form of activity, are:

◆ The Citizenship Foundation, which provides a wide range of competitions to benefit pupils, helping them to extend their knowledge of society and develop leadership and public speaking skills. The Foundation runs competitions such as the Bar and Magistrates' Mock Trial Competitions, to allow pupils to develop some understanding of legal proceedings. Pupils adopt the role of court staff, witnesses and barristers in order to try cases; and have the opportunity to visit Crown or Magistrates' courts as part of the proceedings. The Foundation also runs a mock Parliament Competition and other linked events.

- There is a wide range of debating competitions available to schools; often the local Rotary group will run debating or public speaking competitions. *The Observer* Mace Debating Competition is held each year and the Bright Ideas Group also offer workshops and competitions for public speaking. The Oxford and Cambridge Debating Societies also organize schools' competitions.

- Nationally, the Maths Challenge is well recognized as a competition which allows pupils to develop their mental agility in dealing with mathematical problems in a competitive arena. Similarly the Science Challenge, which is committed to raising awareness of the opportunities offered in terms of careers in the scientific arena.

- Other activities allow pupils to experience the world of business and commerce, for example a competition in which pupils manage their own share portfolios and aim to maximize the profits they make; or Young Enterprise, where pupils run their own businesses.

There are a great many organizations and groups which offer support, advice and competitions to develop more able pupils. Creative writing and poetry competitions as well as engineering challenges are offered to schools throughout the academic year; involvement in these is often rewarding for both pupils and staff.

Creating a culture of success

The process of identifying and highlighting able, gifted and talented pupils can be fraught with difficulty. There are those who object to the identification of the more able and feel it is divisive and unjust. It is important to recognize that the more able child has just as much right to an appropriate education as any other child in school. Providing challenge and encouragement to more able pupils in school is of benefit to *all* pupils. As previously noted, when pupils with a talent in one particular area are taken into account along with those who are gifted in several subject areas, as much as 40 per cent of the school population may be part of the able, gifted and talented programme. It is therefore important that a school creates an ethos which celebrates achievement and success in all its manifestations. This may be achieved in a number of ways.

- Assemblies can be used to highlight individual and group academic, as well as social, success. Sporting achievements and community care achievements are often highlighted, but making academic success a regular focus of celebration is just as important.

- Sending home letters of praise or postcards each term or half term to the parents of those pupils who are considered to have 'achieved' in some element of school life is another method of celebrating success. This tends to be popular with older pupils, who may feel that a 'merit' system is too public, but who do want their parents to be aware of their achievements.

♦ Ensuring that pupils do have a voice in the school, and that their views and needs are elicited. All pupils, not just the more able, need to see themselves as partners in the learning process; if learning itself becomes a priority for a school, rather than solely focusing on subject examination success, pupils tend to place more value on achievement in the classroom.

Key Messages from Chapter 2

♦ Ensure that there is a clear policy for the identification of able, gifted and talented children outlining how the school intends to meet their needs and ensure that they progress.

♦ Make the policy public to all stakeholders.

♦ Appoint a Gifted and Talented Coordinator, or a member of staff with specific responsibility for this group of pupils.

♦ Create a job specification for the Gifted and Talented Coordinator which clearly defines the role. Make plain the expectations of the role and be realistic about what can be achieved.

♦ Consider whether the organization of the school, in terms of classroom teaching and delivery, will allow staff to provide for able, gifted and talented pupils.

♦ Raise awareness of the value of extra-curricular activities and enrichment programmes. The school may well offer a range of activities which can be linked into the able, gifted and talented programme without any additional workload.

- Aim to create a culture of success across the whole school, celebrating achievement in all areas and involving pupils in the learning process.

3

Teaching and Learning: Creating Challenge in the Classroom

'If nobody asked a question, what would the answer be?'

(Gertrude Stein)

The inclusive curriculum

The key question facing all schools as they tackle the issue of providing for able, gifted and talented pupils within the classroom situation is: how should we modify and develop our school's curriculum in order to provide for this specific group of pupils?

In many schools, as we have seen in Chapter 2, there has been a whole-school emphasis on the development of enrichment and extra-curricular activities. This often entails withdrawing nominated able, gifted and/or talented pupils from the normal timetable for a specific period, in order to involve them in a range of activities that will extend their problem solving and creative abilities, their leadership skills, or their expertise in particular subject areas. There is real value in allowing able, gifted and talented pupils a variety of opportunities to engage in activities outside the normal curriculum, not least because they are then working and socializing with pupils of similar abilities and interests. This is a particularly important issue with able underachievers, who often perceive able and motivated pupils as 'geeks'; and therefore need to work alongside these motivated pupils if their misconceptions are to be challenged. However, extending the most able in school cannot be solely a 'bolt on' process of enrichment and extension. In order to achieve a curriculum that is truly inclusive, and that motivates and stimulates our most able pupils, extension through challenge should be fully integrated into lesson planning across the age and subject boundaries. As Eyre and Lowe (2002) have shown, providing for our most able pupils is not a matter of creating an alternative curriculum, but of ensuring that the normal school curriculum meets the needs of all pupils; including the able, gifted and talented.

It has become increasingly clear that the introduction of the National Curriculum, with the attendant focus on levels of attainment and on School League Tables, has led to an emphasis on the teaching of the **content** of the curriculum and to a lack of 'risk taking' in the classroom. Many teachers have confessed to feeling disempowered. They have questioned their own innate awareness of effective teaching and learning strategies; often at the expense of actively involving pupils in their own learning, and raising learners' awareness of the overriding importance of those transferable skills that enable learners to apply their knowledge in new situations. The re-emergence of creativity and originality in the curriculum shown in the Primary Strategy's 'Excellence and Enjoyment' and in developments in the Key Stage 3 Strategy, should enable all teachers to plan for a curriculum that is interesting, that stimulates enquiry and that is, above all, enjoyable. We all learn best when we are having fun; this applies to everybody, including our most able pupils.

What is 'challenge in the classroom'?

At the heart of inclusion are three principles which state that all schools must:

- set suitable learning challenges for all pupils;

- actively engage in overcoming any potential barriers to learning;

- respond to all pupils' diverse needs.

These principles outline clearly the issue that faces teachers every day in the classroom; how do we, as teachers, ensure that we have met the needs of all our pupils through setting suitable learning challenges in the many and varied contexts in which we teach?

There is no one answer to this question. However it is important to remember that a classroom environment that has high expectations of achievement, and provides challenge for the most able pupils, is likely to provide challenge for pupils of all abilities – hence raising achievement and self-esteem for all. It is crucial that teachers find strategies to 'open pupils up' rather than 'shut them down'; thus eliminating any artificial ceilings on learning. The DfES guidelines entitled, 'Excellence and Enjoyment: learning and teaching in the primary years', list six principles for 'achieving the highest possible standards, within a curriculum that motivates and engages them (the pupils)'. These principles cut to the core of effective teaching across the age and ability ranges; and it is unquestionably true that able, gifted and talented pupils are more likely to thrive in a learning climate that:

- sets high expectations and gives every learner confidence they can succeed;

- establishes what learners already know and builds on that knowledge;

- structures and paces the learning experience to make it challenging and enjoyable;

- inspires learning through passion for the subject;

- makes individuals active partners in their learning;

- develops learning skills and personal qualities.

Metacognition – thinking about thinking

A heightened awareness of both teachers' and pupils' use of language in the classroom is a vital part of ensuring that we are meeting the learning needs of our most able pupils. Pupils must be given the linguistic tools they need in order to enhance their awareness of their own thinking processes. Research has shown that able learners have, to a high degree, the ability to reflect on their thinking processes (metacognition), to self-evaluate and to monitor their own thinking in increasingly sophisticated ways. They need to be encouraged to do this; to see the importance of perseverance and of applying new skills creatively in different circumstances, so that learning becomes an overt rather than an implicit process. In addition, it is vitally important for able learners to experience 'failure' in order to appreciate that it is an integral part of the learning process. They need to learn how to learn, and should be given every opportunity to experience a range of different strategies for thinking through and even around the obstacles to success, rather than achieving success effortlessly. It is important that teachers clarify the fact that we never stop learning, and that nobody has the answer to every question; we are all learners together.

Strategies for increasing pupils' metacognitive abilities

Learning logs

Encourage pupils to keep a notebook in which they are given time to record and reflect on the different thinking and problem solving strategies they use in lessons, preferably across the curriculum. They need to evaluate the effectiveness of specific strategies in a variety of learning situations; and begin to make considered decisions about the most efficient strategy to choose in order to successfully complete a task. In this way pupils increase their ability to recognize their own learning styles and strengths, and appreciate the importance of transferring skills across the curriculum. We must ensure that our pupils approach learning as a holistic experience, rather than viewing each subject in its own little 'box', isolated from any other subject.

Concept mapping and mind mapping

These strategies help learners to organize their ideas visually; they are sometimes called graphic organizers.

A **concept map** is a form of web diagram that represents a central idea, and the questions or links associated with that idea. The links are labelled and the direction of thought is denoted with an arrow symbol.

A **mind map** usually consists of one central word or concept. Around that one idea the learner draws branches leading to each of the four or five separate ideas associated with that word or concept. The learner then takes each of these ideas and again draws branches leading to the three or four ideas associated with each one.

Both of these activities encourage learners to explore the interconnectedness between ideas, and to make these connections overt rather than implicit. They allow learners to think laterally rather than in a linear fashion, and to develop their own 'style'.

Verbalizing the thinking process as it takes place

Encouraging pairs or groups of learners to talk through their thinking processes as the thoughts occur during the exploration of a problem, often helps them to slow down and explore other potentially valuable avenues of thought. This is particularly helpful to those more able pupils who are sometimes impatient with collaborative learning. They need to engage in strategies that enable them to see the power of sharing ideas and listening to other people.

Debriefing during and at the end of a task or a sequence of lessons

It is important that pupils are encouraged to reflect on the processes of learning as a natural part of their education, and that they are seen as partners in the learning process rather than as 'little vessels' waiting to be filled with knowledge. Teachers should encourage analysis and discussion about the relative success of learning strategies. They should be explicit in their recognition of pupils' success in using a strategy. A comment such as, 'This group has devised a method for everybody to voice their ideas without interruption – would you like to share it with the rest of the class?' immediately raises the profile of the learning and sharing process, rather than the content of the group discussion. A learning plenary that focuses on skills rather than content helps all pupils, including the most able, to evaluate their strengths and areas for development in terms of thinking processes.

Questioning skills: involvement for teachers and pupils

Effective questioning, leading to progress in learning in the classroom, is an essential skill that needs to be developed by both teachers and pupils. Young children ask innumerable questions as they explore

Creating Challenge in the Classroom

the complexities of everyday life; it is a sad but true fact that this thirst for answers and for further knowledge tends to disappear as children progress through our educational system. It is an interesting, enlightening yet worrying activity to track an able secondary age pupil through a typical school day, noting the number of 'learning' questions that the pupil asks; as opposed to functional questions such as whether to underline headings or which page to use. Often the learning questions are limited to one or two across a school day; in the worst cases none are asked. This justifies the view that many of our learners tend to view themselves as passive recipients of knowledge, rather than active partners in the learning process. In order to enable all pupils, including the able, gifted and talented to attain their full potential, there needs to be a focus on creating a questioning classroom where the teacher's questions extend and probe pupil's responses; and where pupils are explicitly taught how to question in order to build on responses and explore ideas.

There are many ways of involving pupils more fully in their own learning through a much greater emphasis on questioning, thereby allowing pupils to take more responsibility for their progress. Several of these are outlined below.

KWL Grid. This stands for: What do I know; What do I want or need to know? What have I learned?

At the beginning of a topic, ask pupils to discuss and to note down in bullet points what they already know about the topic. This enables the teacher to investigate prior learning. Follow this by asking pupils, again in pairs, to write down the questions that **they** would like to ask about the topic about to be studied; these questions should be shared and discussed with the class and then retained, either by the teacher or by the pupils. The questions should be reviewed with the class at the end of the topic, to see if their questions have been answered. This strategy is effective in drawing pupils into a topic and giving them much greater ownership of it.

The same technique works effectively at the end of a lesson. Ask the pupils to write down any questions they may have about the material covered in the lesson; collect them in, and ensure that any queries or misconceptions are answered in the course of the next lesson.

Given the answer/s, learners devise the questions

The majority of question and answer sessions in the typical classroom are led by the teacher, as questioner, with the pupils giving the answers. Much more precise and detailed thinking can be encouraged if pupils are asked to work out the possible questions that would elicit a given answer. Instead of setting test questions, give the pupils the answers; ask the pupils in pairs or groups to work out potential examination questions on a given topic, and justify their ideas. Devising questions entails looking at a subject from a different point of view, and often requires an essential understanding of success criteria.

Play 'games' that will extend pupils' understanding of questioning skills

Activities such as Twenty Questions, Find Your Partner or lateral thinking puzzles, are valuable learning strategies.

In **Twenty Questions**, pupils have Post-Its placed on their backs or signs above their heads telling the rest of the class what they are. For example, one pupil, or a pair of pupils, might represent a rat that brought the plague to England in the Middle Ages. The pupil or pupils have to ask questions of the rest of the class or group, to try to find out what they are; the limit is twenty questions.

In **Find Your Partner** the teacher puts labels on the pupils' backs, which clearly show what or who they represent. Each pupil should ultimately be able to find one or more partners. So, for example, the topic might be scientists and their discoveries. The pupils representing the scientists must find out who they are, by asking questions of all the other pupils with yes or no answers; once they know who they are, they then pair up with the pupil who represents the discovery the scientist made – and vice versa.

Lateral thinking puzzles, in which the pupils have to follow sequences of questions rather than immediately start guessing the answer can be effective and enjoyable starter activities.

Restructure the start of the lesson

Many lessons begin with a review of previous learning that relies on teacher-led questions and pupil answers; often this may involve only a few pupils, or result in quick-fire question and answer that does not allow for the development of ideas. The beginning of a lesson is the most effective time for thinking and learning, therefore it makes sense to involve as many pupils as possible by setting them the challenge of creating the questions to review learning, and asking each other. This can become a competition, particularly if the pupils work collaboratively.

The Classroom Climate

In order to create a classroom climate where questioning is valued as a skill to be developed as part of independent learning, it is important for the teacher to build a secure learning environment in which pupils are willing to take risks without fear of peer pressure or being 'put down'. We need to value all sorts of answers to open questions as 'good thinking' and valid, rather than only giving credit for the answer on the teacher's agenda at that moment. We must ensure that our pupils are secure in the knowledge that not immediately succeeding at a task, or answering a question 'wrongly', is not a failure in itself but an essential part of exploratory learning. Too many of our pupils fail to realize that there is not always a right or a wrong answer, and that it is often the thinking processes themselves that are more important. The following strategies, when practised in a classroom over a period of time, can help to create that ethos of safety in which teachers and pupils learn in partnership.

- When questioning pupils, allow brief thinking time, or talk time with a partner – even 30 seconds can make all the difference to our pupils' sense of security and willingness to respond.

- Rather than relying on quick-fire question and answer sessions in which the majority of pupils give very limited responses, encourage individual pupils to extend responses by asking, for example, 'Why do you think that?' or 'How did you arrive at that idea?' Draw in the rest of the class by asking, 'Who else would agree with that idea? Why?'

- Encourage pupils to justify their responses, for example by asking, 'What is the evidence for that idea? Can you give me three reasons why we might think that?'

- Try not to shut down pupils' questions because of the pressure of time. Able pupils in particular find it frustrating to be told 'You don't need to know that now' or 'We don't have time to think about that now'. They ask questions because they do need to know; and should be given some idea of how to find an answer; including pointers for individual research, if the matter is impossible to discuss in class at that moment. A few words with the teacher at the end of the lesson will often help to direct the pupil further, and ease any sense of dissatisfaction.

Explicit teaching of questioning skills

Pupils need to know the difference between open and closed questions, and how to move from concrete and literal questions to those that explore abstracts and concepts. This does require a whole-class focus, and one framework that engages both teachers and pupils in recognizing the level of their questioning and thinking, is through developing strategies to increase the use of the higher order thinking skills as defined by Benjamin Bloom (1956).

Bloom's Taxonomy of Thinking Skills

In 1956 Benjamin Bloom led a team of educational psychologists who developed a classification of the levels of thinking that are important in learning.

Bloom's Taxonomy defines six levels of human thinking skills. The first three levels are often termed the 'lower order' skills as they rely on recognizing and recalling information, organizing and arranging material, and applying previously learned information to reach a conclusion. The three 'higher level' skills require pupils to think critically and creatively, to evaluate, and to transfer skills and knowledge from one situation to another. It is the higher level skills that we particularly want our able, gifted and talented pupils to access; however all pupils should be given opportunities to access these skills as an integral part of their learning development. Bloom found in 1956 that 95 per cent of teachers' questions targeted the lower order skills; enhancing both teachers' and pupils' knowledge of the taxonomy helps to ensure that our own classrooms allow pupils to analyse, to synthesize and to evaluate across the curriculum.

In some classrooms Bloom's Taxonomy, or the 'building blocks' of thinking as it is sometimes known, is displayed and referred to routinely throughout lessons by both teachers and pupils. Integrating the different levels of thinking skills into planning is a simple yet effective method for ensuring that pupils are given those vital opportunities to access the higher order skills.

Table 1. Bloom's Taxonomy of Thinking Skills

Competence	Skills	Useful verbs	Question stems
Knowledge	Memorize Remember Recognize Recall	List, identify, tell, define, label, name, collect	Who … ? What … ? When … ? Where … ? Describe what happened … ? How many … ?
Compre-hension	Interpret Organize and select Translate from one medium to another Identify	Summarize, explain, paraphrase, illustrate, estimate, distinguish, predict	Can you retell the story … ? Can you provide an example of … ? Can you predict … ? Estimate how many … ?
Application	Use information Solve problems using required skills or knowledge	Apply, demonstrate, discover, modify, classify, calculate,	Can you apply this to … ? What questions would you ask of … ? Make up a set

Able, Gifted and Talented

Competence	Skills	Useful verbs	Question stems
	Use methods/ concepts/ theories in new situations	complete, solve, experiment	of instructions for ... ? Could this have happened in ... ?
Analysis	Seeing patterns Organization of parts Recognition of hidden meanings Identification of components Identify facts and fallacies	Connect, select, analyse, compare, arrange, divide, categorize, order	What was the turning point ... ? Why do you think ... ? Which comments are true ... ? Can you distinguish between ... ?
Synthesis	Use old ideas to create new Predict and draw conclusions Relate knowledge from several areas Generalize from given facts	Assess, recommend, modify, rewrite, create, compose, construct, invent, predict, argue, forecast, design	Can you design a ... ? Can you compose a new ... ? What would happen if ... ? How many ways can you ... ?
Evaluation ... ?	Compare and discriminate between ideas Assess the value of ideas	Judge, select, choose, recommend, prioritize, rank, grade,	How effective are ... ? Can you prioritize and rank order ... ? What criteria

Competence	Skills	Useful verbs	Question stems
	Develop opinions and judgements Make choices based on reasoned argument	determine, debate, assess, verify, justify, evaluate	would you use to assess ... ? Can you justify your decision ... ?

The Norman Conquest: An outline plan using Bloom's Taxonomy (History)

Knowledge

- When did the Norman Conquest take place?

- Traditionally, how do we believe that Harold died?

Comprehension

- Draw up a timeline showing the major events leading up to the Norman Conquest, from 1000 AD onwards.

Application

- In groups, think about the questions that you might have asked Harold, had you been able to interview him before the Battle of Hastings.

Analysis

- Examine the three source extracts and list any evidence you find that indicates Harold's responsibility for the defeat of the English at the Battle of Hastings.

Synthesis

♦ Write the lost letter that Harold sent to William three months before William's invasion of England. In this letter, Harold tries to prove to William that he can never win the crown of England and has no real claim to it.

Evaluation

♦ What would have been the consequences (long-term and short-term) if Harold had won the Battle of Hastings?

♦ Can the invasion of another country ever be justified?

Thinking about planning in this way can be helpful when trying to ensure that all pupils are adequately challenged in the classroom. Some teachers plan lessons according to these guidelines – calling it the **Must, Should, Could** technique. In other words, in this lesson or sequence of lessons, what **must** all of my pupils undertake and understand; what **should** they all undertake and understand; and what **could** my most able pupils undertake and understand.

The social context for learning – speaking, listening, collaborative learning

There has been a relatively recent recognition that most pupils' thinking and understanding can be dramatically enhanced if they are given structured and well managed opportunities for collaborative work within and outside the classroom. Pupils need to be given opportunities to explore their learning through dialogue and discussion with one another; thereby extending their linguistic skills and vocabulary, the metacognitive processing of the learning taking place, and their ability to work with others in a variety of different contexts. The latter point is very important for those able, gifted and talented pupils who are sometimes impatient of, and disparaging about, other people's abilities; and would prefer to complete every task on their own. They do need to acquire the social and emotional skills that will enable them to function effectively in the outside world.

Speaking, listening and collaborative activities are also extremely important because they provide another forum in which pupils can demonstrate their real and potential abilities. Many of our summative assessment activities depend on the written word and pupils' abilities to perform well in written assessments. Not all pupils respond positively to these types of assessment activities. Some may lack motivation and fail to see the point of the activity, therefore making little effort; others may have specific learning difficulties, such as dyslexia, that make written responses particularly difficult. Through discussion and dialogue with others, pupils are able to demonstrate their capabilities in problem solving and creative and critical thinking. Self-esteem and the pupils' self-image can be raised if teachers overtly value speaking, listening and collaborative abilities on a par with written activities and outcomes. It should not be possible in future for pupils to go home and tell their parents, 'Oh we didn't do any work in school today, we just talked'.

Collaborative work in the classroom can be

structured in a number of ways, through pairs and groups. Some ideas have already been outlined in the section on questioning. The teacher does need to facilitate and manage the work if it is to be truly effective; and the pupils need to be given opportunities to make choices, to take on specific roles, and to evaluate their speaking, listening and collaborative skills as well as the learning outcomes of their work. This will, in turn, increase pupils' confidence in articulating and justifying ideas. The QCA materials, Speaking and Listening in Key Stages 1 and 2, give a range of good ideas for structured collaborative work that can be readily adapted for Key Stages 3, 4 and 5. The following points outline some strategies that can be helpful in creating structured group-work.

◆ Ask pupils to discuss and allocate specific roles within the group: for example, chairperson; scribe; spokesperson; timekeeper; artist. Clearly the roles will vary according to the task set. It is often a good idea to appoint an observer, either to one or to all groups. This person, following clear criteria, observes the group interaction and reports back at the end of the process, thus giving feedback on the groups' strengths and areas for development.

◆ Snowballing is a process in which the pupils are initially asked to consider a question individually and note down some ideas. They then share those ideas with a partner; the pair then becomes a group of four, and then a group of eight. In this way ideas are shared and pooled; additional challenge is created when the larger group is perhaps asked to decide which three, of all the ideas, are the most important/relevant/useful; and then to rank order them.

- ◆ Jigsaw grouping allows pupils to become 'experts' in a subject, and then to teach pupils in another group using their expertise. Teaching others is the most effective way of learning because the knowledge and information has to be re-ordered and transformed so that others will understand. For this activity the teacher should divide the class into groups, and allocate each group one specific aspect of a topic to research. Having completed their research and pooled their findings, each group is numbered off, and the pupils then form new groups according to their numbers. Each pupil then shares his or her expert knowledge with the rest of the new group, leading towards a specified outcome.

It is vital that pupils are asked to work within a range of different pupil groupings, rather than solely with their friends or within ability groups. Groups that are deliberately structured by the teacher to optimize not only academic ability, but character and personality strengths and areas for development, will support differentiation and pupils' holistic development. Able, gifted and talented pupils are not necessarily good leaders; and need to be given opportunities within a secure environment to develop that quality. Teachers must also ensure that they use all available data and other relevant information about the individual pupils they teach when planning collaborative work, as well as when planning written activities; and the information should be used from the time that a teacher first takes over a new class or teaching group.

Assessment for learning

Formative assessment, or assessment for learning as it is more commonly known, has been shown to have significant effects both in raising pupils' standards of attainment (Black and Wiliam 1998) and in increasing their self-esteem. Many of the features of assessment for learning, including questioning skills and collaborative learning, have already been covered in this chapter. Formative assessment means that pupils become partners in their own learning, understanding not only why they are learning, but how to make progress and become increasingly independent of teacher direction. This is a key factor in the education of able, gifted and talented pupils; and particularly so for able underachievers, who often feel that they are the passive recipients of knowledge and that they have little personal involvement or responsibility in the education process. Formative assessment depends on the teacher creating a dialogue with and between pupils, which is supportive and enables them to have an element of choice in their learning.

Key features of assessment for learning

◆ learning objectives are made clear to pupils and success criteria are established; preferably in partnership with the pupils;

- learning, as distinct from task outcomes, is reviewed at the end of a lesson or a sequence of lessons;

- oral and written feedback enables pupils to understand what they have achieved, where they are in their learning, and how to take the next steps for progress;

- pupils are involved in both peer and self-assessment, therefore the success criteria must be shared and understood, and pupils have time to reflect upon their learning;

- pupils are encouraged to set achievable targets, in partnership with the teacher;

- teachers and pupils work together to create a climate of success in the classroom.

Creating a classroom ethos where assessment for learning works effectively does not happen overnight, however there are ways in which teachers can help to make it successful. These include:

- Explain why pupils are being involved in the assessment process, and the WIIFM factor – 'What's in it for me'. Able pupils like to understand the 'big picture' and the reasons for doing things in certain ways.

- Talk to pupils about their learning and about their learning experiences. Encourage them to reflect on how they learn most effectively, and what stops them from learning. Able underachievers, in particular, need to be encouraged to view learning as an active process that will have an impact on their lives in the future.

♦ Avoid grading or levelling every piece of work; give these at intervals during the school year, or for specified pieces of work. Pupils need to know the stage they have reached, but an over-reliance on grades and levels detracts from any diagnostic comments and can create a climate of unhealthy competition and a sense of failure.

♦ Involve pupils in generating success and assessment criteria, particularly when establishing peer- and self-assessment. Give pupils psychological strategies for peer-assessment such as the 'critical sandwich' – a positive comment, followed by an improvement comment; followed by another positive comment.

♦ Ensure that pupils are aware of the success criteria before they begin a piece of work. In English, for example, they need to know that not every piece of work is being assessed for spelling and handwriting!

♦ Avoid using the word 'but' when writing comments; however positive the comment may be, learners tend to focus on the comment that comes after 'but'.

All learners need to know how to make progress. It is tempting, as a teacher, to simply write 'Excellent' on a very able pupil's work; and to feel that we have given adequate feedback through praise because there is nothing else to say. However, able, gifted and talented pupils do need to have more developed and progressive feedback from their teachers. If a pupil in Year 7 generally receives nothing but praise across the curriculum, are we really saying that he or she can make no further progress in the next six years of schooling?

ICT, multi media and able, gifted and talented pupils

ICT is a powerful tool for learning, and our most able pupils need to be encouraged to take the opportunities that are opened up to them through the range of uses of ICT. As teachers, we must bear in mind the fact that effective ICT skills will be a necessity for most forms of employment in the future. We should also be aware that ICT allows pupils different forms of access to problem-solving and creativity, and can therefore be a highly motivational tool when used for these purposes in the classroom. In addition to this, ICT and multi media resources can open up a whole new world to pupils, and allow them to make links with other organizations, with professionals and with pupils in countries across the globe; therefore enhancing their awareness of the potential real applications of their learning. Some of the ways that ICT can be used effectively with able, gifted and talented pupils are outlined below.

- Set up email links with pupils and teachers in other schools. Rather than 'social' links, ensure that the pupils work together in designing, planning, writing and problem-solving. Encourage them to act as response partners to one another. Many able pupils tend to put more effort into their work when they have a real audience, other than the teacher.

- More schools now have access to video conferencing facilities, and these can provide stimulating opportunities for pupils to engage in dialogue with professionals. For example, The Globe Theatre in London asks groups of pupils to adopt an actor, and offers the pupils the facility to interview their actor via video conferencing. Through The British Council, schools can develop multi-media links with schools abroad.

- Able pupils can be encouraged to produce a school newspaper that focuses not only on local news, but gives critical opinions and thoughts about events across the world. They will need to use appropriate internet resources and websites.

- Computer simulations can be effective ways of engaging pupils in potentially real situations, such as electioneering and advertising campaigns.

Many teachers still have a slightly uneasy awareness that some of their pupils are more skilled users of ICT than they are. It is important to utilize, and to celebrate, the expertise that so many of our pupils are now developing. Involving more able pupils in teaching and coaching others who are less confident ICT users is one way of developing the learning skills of all concerned; and creates the senses of responsibility, independence and reality that are necessary for a number of our most able pupils.

Listening to able, gifted and talented pupils

Throughout this book, we have commented on the importance of opening up a dialogue with able pupils – those who are on track to achieve their potential, and those who may currently lack motivation or direction. It is only by talking to these pupils, and finding out what they think and believe about their own learning experiences through their school careers, that we can really help to make a difference on an individual level. The responses outlined in this section have been repeated in interviews and conversations with able pupils of all ages over the last few years, and therefore represent a distillation of their comments.

◆ Avoid asking able pupils to do 'more of the same' just because they are recognized as being able. Why should an able pupil be expected to write four pages while the rest of the class writes two pages? Or to complete an extra worksheet? The most common way for able pupils to get around this teacher tactic is to write more slowly and waste as much time as possible; this can become a habit!

◆ Able pupils express discontent with the feelings of boredom and frustration that can mount up when they feel that the work they are asked to do is too easy, and lacks the real challenge that puts them just outside their 'comfort zone' in terms of thinking and problem-solving. The majority of able pupils who are 'cruising' in school are well aware of the fact, and know how to do just enough to get by. They are also aware that if they are not challenged in the classroom, they can become lazy and disinclined to make much effort – unless the topic really interests them.

♦ Able pupils may dislike responses to questions that disallow wide-ranging enquiry or lateral thinking. If they ask a question, it is important to them in terms of making progress in their learning, and they need at least to be told how to try to find an answer. They are aware when teachers are, as one pupil phrased it, 'teaching to an agenda'; and when the teachers are unwilling or unable to digress from that agenda.

♦ Able boys in particular express dissatisfaction with being expected to complete homework that is simply being used to fill in the homework time. They need homework tasks that fulfil a clear learning purpose and enable them to make progress in the acquisition of skills or knowledge.

♦ The development of research skills, and opportunities to undertake focused research, are valued by able pupils. They are able to take more responsibility, and to follow lines of enquiry that interest them. It is important that all pupils are taught to research effectively, and to transform the information they acquire for a specific purpose.

♦ Able pupils who are, or have been, shy or withdrawn, comment on the feelings of resentment that arise when their ability is not recognized by their teachers simply because they are quiet and unwilling to 'expose' themselves in class. This is a pattern that can continue for a number of years, with consequent damage to the pupil's self-esteem.

- Some able pupils find it very difficult to organize themselves; to take the correct books to lessons, to meet deadlines and even to complete work at all. These pupils often do benefit from being assigned a mentor who will coach them in study skills and how to prioritize, particularly if they lead very busy lives outside of school.

- Many able pupils are reluctant to be withdrawn from their classes to join what may be seen by their peers, by staff, and by parents as an elite group. They often prefer not to be singled out as they can be worried about peer pressure, jealousy and even bullying. They can be very resentful if they are withdrawn from activities, subjects and teachers that they like. Able children do enjoy working with others of like abilities; however the forum for this to occur should help them to feel secure and valued, rather than exposed.

- Surprisingly, a large number of able pupils are unaware that they are, or might potentially be, able, gifted or talented. Pupils who have been invited to attend gifted and talented summer schools will sometimes confess that they don't feel they are good enough. Even their parents can be surprised. The self-esteem of these unaware yet able pupils rises significantly when they know that their potential has been identified.

Key Messages from Chapter 3

- Challenging able, gifted and talented pupils should be an integral part of the everyday learning experience across the curriculum, rather than depending on specific enrichment, withdrawal or acceleration activities.

- Able, gifted and talented pupils value opportunities to become more fully involved in their own learning processes; and thus begin to understand that learning should be a pro-active process.

- Able, gifted and talented pupils need to experience 'failure' as an essential part of the learning process. They need to be encouraged to explore different avenues of thought, and to realize that there is not always a 'right' or 'wrong' answer.

- Pupils must be given opportunities to participate in activities in the classroom that will enable them to show their true ability. Oral, rather than written responses, may provide evidence of real abilities.

- Pupils need to be taught the value of questioning, and how to question effectively. They must be allowed opportunities to practise their questioning skills across the curriculum and in a safe environment, knowing that their contributions will be valued and that lines of enquiry will be opened up rather than closed down.

- Pupils often learn best through structured discussion and exploration of ideas with each other and with the teacher.

Creating Challenge in the Classroom

- Adding challenge to the learning situation in the classroom through targeting the higher-order thinking skills is of immense benefit, not only to more able pupils, but to pupils of all abilities and ages.

- Able, gifted and talented pupils value and enjoy activities that enable them to think creatively and originally, encouraging independence in learning.

- Teachers need to be aware of the importance of their own language use in the classroom; as a model for pupils, and to enable pupils to extend their own language skills in order to gain access to more complex thinking and problem-solving.

- Pupils should be encouraged to discuss the links between learning in different areas of the curriculum so that they view learning experiences holistically, rather than as isolated subject areas.

- Able, gifted and talented pupils should be encouraged to use all available tools for learning, including ICT and multi media.

4

The Involvement of Parents and Governors

It is crucial to gain support from both parents and school governors in order to enhance the provision for able, gifted and talented pupils. Regular contact with interested parties can provide very valuable links into the local community and support for enrichment in a number of ways.

The parents of gifted and talented pupils

Most parents are supportive of any work that the school undertakes with their children and take an extremely active interest in the development of their child and the provision made for them. It is important to remember that any provision for able, gifted and talented pupils must take account of social and emotional needs as well as intellectual needs, and this must be fully understood by the parents. Nevertheless, parents do have a right to know if their child is considered to be, or to have the potential to be, gifted or talented. Parents also need to be informed quickly if their potentially more able child is considered to be underachieving in one or more areas of the curriculum; there is nothing more frustrating to a parent than to be given such information at the end of a school year, when valuable time may have been lost and the patterns of underachievement have been set. It may be that membership of an outside organization, such as the National Academy for Gifted and Talented Youth (NAGTY), can give a child the necessary motivation to succeed in school; parents need to be aware of the support networks that are available to them and to their children. However, tensions between teachers and parents can appear at times regarding the provision made for the more able, and these can be summarized as outlined below.

Staff may feel that parents:

- have unrealistic expectations of the provision that schools make in dealing with able, gifted and talented pupils;

- believe that their child is able, gifted or talented based solely on their knowledge of their own child and without any basis for comparison;

- perceive that enrichment programmes outside of the classroom are the only ones that can adequately challenge their child; they are perhaps unaware of the significance of daily classroom provision;

- will be 'difficult' if their child's potential fails to develop as initially expected.

The issues can often be resolved simply through effective communication between the school and the parents. The Gifted and Talented Coordinator, or the member of staff nominated for more able provision, should be the point of contact between the two interested parties. This need not necessarily be an onerous or time-consuming process. There are a number of simple and efficient ways of providing parents with information and updates that will help them to be aware of the school's provision.

- It may be useful in the first term of the academic year to hold an open evening for interested parents, to inform them about effective teaching and learning. This need not be aimed solely at the parents of more able children but should be an open invitation to all parents. The evening can be used to highlight the changing nature of classroom delivery, through workshop sessions providing practical activities designed to demonstrate proven methods for raising pupil attainment, and how differentiation and challenge are built into lessons. It should be made clear that pupils benefit from a variety of approaches to learning, for example through planning for the full range of pupils' learning styles and challenging thinking skills. This should allow parents to see that challenge for all pupils comes from a variety of sources; and that provision within the classroom for the more able pupils is ultimately more important than the enrichment programme the school may offer.

- A school may wish to trial sending letters home to the parents of pupils identified as more able, making them aware of the fact that their child has been recognized by the school, and in what capacity. It is interesting to note that parents are often unaware of the fact that their child is considered to be able, gifted or talented and are delighted to learn that the identification process has taken place. In addition, if at all possible, include a programme of enrichment activities that will occur during the year. This will serve to highlight to parents the range of activities that may be on offer to their child. It is essential to point out that not every activity will be suitable for every identified pupil; nor is it possible for the same pupils to be included in all of the activities provided during the year. Following up the letters with a meeting in which more detailed information can be given, including specific identification issues, helps to create the essential dialogue between the school and the parents.

♦ Ensure that the parents of children invited to attend gifted and talented summer schools are aware of why their child has been invited and, even more importantly, how the summer school experience will be followed up within the school environment. This can be a very contentious issue. The majority of pupils enjoy a gifted and talented summer school and gain a great deal in terms of motivation and self-confidence. If the child's progress in not then monitored in school, and the majority of staff are unaware that the child attended the summer school, parents quite rightly begin to feel that there is a lack of communication and forward planning regarding their child's progress in school.

♦ Ask parents to provide additional information

about their more able child, as parents know their children far better than teachers and can be a vital source of additional data. This is particularly important at transition points between Key Stages where progression is absolutely essential. See Appendix 2 for an example of the sort of questions it may be useful to ask.

♦ Some schools involve parents in the initial identification process of able, gifted and talented pupils. This can be achieved by writing to parents and asking them to nominate their child with any justification that they feel is appropriate. While for some staff this may seem a slightly 'risky' process, it can be very useful. Parents are usually honest and accurate in their analysis of their own children; but the process should be handled sensitively and with care.

♦ Involve parents in supporting able, gifted and talented pupils in school. If parents are willing to volunteer their services they may often be helpful in working with small groups of able pupils, or delivering a self-contained unit or enrichment activity in which they have specialist knowledge. Parents may also be able to provide links with the wider community, involving local businesses or organizations.

Governors

School governors can be extremely supportive in work with able, gifted and talented pupils. Aim to draw on any skills that they may have and encourage them to take an active role in monitoring and evaluating the school's provision.

The governing body of any school has a statutory responsibility for ensuring there is provision for able, gifted and talented pupils. Effective communication is the key here. Keeping the governors informed of the school's policy for dealing with more able pupils and the developments in providing for them is important. Ideally, one governor should be given the role of linking with the Gifted and Talented Coordinator and overseeing this area of the curriculum. The link governor can act as a conduit for information and as an advocate for the interests of the more able pupils in the school.

Providing governors with up-to-date information about the able, gifted and talented in the school, and how provision is made for this group of pupils is essential. Inviting them to join in with parents on a teaching and learning evening can be an enlightening process for the whole governing body. The Gifted and Talented Coordinator should take advantage of opportunities to attend governors' meetings and provide presentations, reports and practical activities in which they can take part. The governors need to understand the requirements of these pupils, and how the school and staff work to provide challenge and stimulation for all the pupils in the school. The processes of identification, and the distinctions between the terms able, gifted and talented, also need to be understood by the governors.

In smaller schools, where staff must take on a variety of different responsibilities, it should be both possible and profitable to liaise with colleagues from other institutions, or to work in clusters to provide training for parents, governors and staff. The benefits of this type of collaboration, for pupils and for teachers, are inestimable. The LEA should also be prepared to provide support and training for governors in a variety of respects. The Gifted and Talented Coordinator, or the member of staff nominated to oversee the provision for the able, gifted and talented, should approach the LEA to see what might be provided in the way of training for those on the governing body who are seeking to understand more about provision for the more able in the mainstream school.

Mentoring

It may be possible to encourage parents and governors to involve themselves in mentoring programmes for more able pupils. This not only has the benefit of reducing the time commitment of staff, but is also especially profitable when the gifted or talented child is mentored by an adult who shares a common interest. It may be possible to offer real-life experience in a particular field and therefore encourage the gifted or talented pupil to pursue an interest or career path. In this way pupils may be able to develop both new and existing skills and to discover their suitability for particular roles. As with any area in which adults from outside school are involved in working with pupils, this activity needs to be carefully structured and monitored. Risk assessments, school and LEA procedures must be adhered to at all times.

Key Messages from Chapter 4

- Communication with parents and governors is absolutely vital and all of the school's procedures for identifying and providing for the able, gifted and talented must be transparent and fair. Ensure that both parents and governors are made aware of what the school provides in the way of support of and the policies for able, gifted and talented pupils, and how individual pupils are receiving this support.

- Have a clear policy for the identification and provision of pupils, make this documentation public and adhere to it closely. In this way, if parents have queries or concerns, or question the school's provision, you can refer them to the policy and reassure them.

- Ensure that parents and governors fully understand the terminology and the issues surrounding the identification and provision for more able, gifted and talented pupils. A real dialogue between the school and the parents/governors should be created, with a central liaison role for the Gifted and Talented Coordinator.

- Provide opportunities for parents and governors to become actively involved in enrichment or support programmes. Elicit their expertise in specific areas. This should provide them with a sense of ownership in that they become stakeholders in the programme.

5

Useful Information and Resources for Teachers and Parents

The World Class Tests

The World Class Tests administered by NFER Nelson are a useful tool for providing additional challenge for more able pupils. There are two separate papers; one in problem-solving, the other in Mathematics. These papers are designed to be sat by pupils aged 8 to 11 in their primary school and by pupils aged 12 to 14 in secondary schools; the suggestion is that the tests are aimed at 9 and 13 year olds. Students need to use logic and reasoning combined with creative problem-solving in order to succeed in these papers. Pupils may sit either one or both examinations and these take the form of written papers and online testing. Pupils need to sit both the written and online elements of the test. It is useful to note, therefore, that pupils will need access to an individual PC under examination conditions and that technical support may be required. Details of the technological requirements can be found on the website (see below). If your school is unable to provide suitable facilities or support it may be possible to enter pupils through a local test centre – often another local school, although this may incur additional charges for administration.

The tests themselves draw on a range of subject areas including Science, Design Technology and Mathematics. The papers are not designed to assess the subject knowledge of pupils, but their ability to use deductive reasoning to solve challenging questions. There is a charge for sitting the papers, these are £7 each for the Mathematics and Problem-solving in the 8–11 age range, and £9 each for the tests aimed at 12 to 14 year olds. Testing currently takes place in the Spring Term, in April, but there are plans to offer more flexible testing opportunities in the future. For more information consult the test website which can be found at www.worldclassarena.org.

Please note: NAGTY accepts the results of the World Class Tests as one of their criteria for entry.

Masterclasses, Challenge Days and Leadership Programmes

Events such as these usually form part of an enrichment programme and may involve pupils being withdrawn from lessons, extra-curricular activities or projects in the holidays. Such activities give the more able pupils the opportunity for widening what is normally taught in the classroom. It can provide the opportunity to cover work of a more difficult standard or more in depth; more time may be given to a particular activity in this environment. Grouping of pupils may be more creative, with pupils from different phases or year groups working together. Pupils can be given the opportunity to work cross-phase with older pupils. Older pupils can be encouraged to mentor younger pupils or act as group leaders. The involvement of the local community or business in these projects can also be very helpful, allowing able, gifted and talented pupils to experience elements of the world of work and challenge in a way not generally provided in school.

Setting up your own enrichment projects can be rewarding. Science Challenge days where pupils undertake a variety of related tasks such as building planes or rockets and considering flight and aero-dynamics, is one such example. Media Challenge Days, in which pupils produce newspapers and/or news programmes, can also be effective enrichment activities. Often these can be based on 'Newstream' type media ICT programmes, where snippets of news are delivered at intervals in order for pupils to assimilate and organize the relevant detail from the information provided. Offering opportunities for pupils to work with a poet or writer for a day can be invaluable. Physical challenges devised for pupils talented in a particular sport can also allow pupils to develop skills not always tackled in the course of a normal school day.

Masterclasses in which 'experts' are invited to lead sessions to encourage pupils of exceptional ability can offer extension far beyond that offered by the regular curriculum. Many enrichment programmes provide superb opportunities for pupils to take on leadership roles, and this is to be encouraged. Leadership of teams can be allowed to evolve naturally, or can be manipulated in order to encourage self-confidence.

It is, however, important to recognize that enrichment activities such as these should be seen very much as supplementary to what goes on in the classroom. They can in no way replace effective and challenging teaching in lessons for more able pupils.

The National Academy for Gifted and Talented Youth (NAGTY)

The National Academy for Gifted and Talented Youth is based at Warwick University and is a government-funded initiative to support and develop the teaching and learning of gifted and talented pupils. Initially it provided for pupils aged between 11 and 16, but from September 2004 the Academy will also become involved, 'in a progressive way', with gifted and talented children of primary school age. The institution also provides support and guidance for teachers and parents, supplying information and advice to assist those who have contact with able pupils.

The Academy aims to focus on those pupils who are in the top 5 per cent of young people and to ensure that their needs are met. A pupil, once registered with the Academy, is able to take advantage of a variety of services they provide, including Gifted and Talented Summer Schools, weekend conferences and courses, and online forums and chat rooms.

There are a number of benefits that NAGTY can offer to the able pupil. Among many young people the idea prevails that being bright is something to be concealed rather than celebrated. Being highlighted as a 'gifted' child may be embarrassing or lead to victimization. The Academy is made up of like-minded individuals of similar ability and therefore pupils feel more comfortable and more likely to gain acceptance in this environment. The Academy is also able to provide challenging opportunities for pupils, often in subject areas that are not available in school. Expert tutors can offer teaching and support in Classics, Ancient History, and Engineering amongst other more unusual subject areas.

A range of criteria may be used to indicate that a pupil is sufficiently able to become a member. Clearly ability is developmental and this is recognized by the Academy; professional recommendation is considered as well as examples of the pupil's work. Detailed lists of suitable evidence for membership are listed on the NAGTY website along with more detailed information. Some of the indicative membership criteria are listed below:

- a score of over 128 on two elements or more of Cognitive Ability Tests (CATs);

- MidYIS/Yellis scores of over 125;

- YELLIS scores of over 70 in Year 10 or 81 in Year 11;

- SATs results at Key Stage 2 which display a pupil working beyond Level 5 in more than one subject area;

- SATs results at Key Stage 3 which display a pupil working beyond Level 7 in more than one subject area;

- A/A* in eight or more subjects at GCSE;

- World Class Tests – distinction;

- examples of a pupil's work which is annotated showing evidence of outstanding achievement.

The Academy also aims to support those involved in the education and development of gifted and talented pupils. It provides In Service Training, online support, conferences, and is a centre of excellence providing examples of best practice and expertise to help to improve the teaching and learning of the more able pupils in schools.

Summer Schools

The opportunity for gifted and talented pupils to attend a Summer School can provide extension and enrichment beyond the classroom. The government encouraged pilot projects for a variety of types of summer schools in 1999 and since then the schemes have been widened, extending to virtually all LEAs and EAZs from 2000 (involving around 14,500 pupils in 2000). LEAs are able to put in bids for funding to run summer schools; how they then utilize the funding varies from area to area but must of course take into account the DfES guidelines.

The aim of Gifted and Talented Summer Schools is to raise the self-esteem of able pupils, to provide them with a safe environment in which to explore their gifts and to encourage personal development and raise achievement. It provides a scheme to extend and enrich the range of academic, social and cultural experiences of pupils while making learning fun. Summer schools may also encourage pupils who do not normally participate in extra-curricular activities to become involved.

Planning a Gifted and Talented Summer School

No guide such as this could hope to provide an extensive list of all the information that you might require in devising a summer school plan. These are simply some suggestions as to how you might approach the process.

◆ Begin to plan very early; you may not receive confirmation of funding until January but you will need to be prepared to progress quickly once the confirmation is received. If you are working with other schools/institutions then the planning process is likely to be more lengthy.

◆ Approach staff who may be interested in partici-pating and ensure that they are willing to devote the required time. It may be possible to include specialists to support the activities, for example writers/poets, artists and scientists. It may also be useful to supplement the teaching staff with volunteers; these may either be drawn from interested parents or older pupils in the school. Remember to ensure that the ratio of staff to pupils is appropriate and that you arrange for payment – usually done through the school payroll. It is important to note that staffing will be a major part of your budget and that this should be carefully accounted for – including caretakers and other support staff who may be required.

- Establish clear criteria for pupils attending the summer school and ask schools to provide data on recommended pupils in order that the selection process is more straightforward. Ensure that it is not simply well-motivated, well-behaved and hard-working pupils who are recommended. It is particularly important to encourage the disaffected and able underachievers to attend.

- Think about the timing of the summer school. This will of course be reliant on the availability of the venue and of the staff. It is, however, often easier to encourage pupils to attend early in the holidays outside of the bank holiday period in August.

- The venue for the summer school is also important. Many summer schools take place in school but it is possible to spend some or all of the time off site in a hired venue; a museum, library or at a residential centre. If you are holding the event in your own school ensure that caretakers and staff who may be affected but are not directly involved, are informed.

- Ensure that you have fulfilled all requirements regarding health and safety, risk assessments and insurance. This can often be a lengthy and time-consuming process but is vitally important.

- Contact parents as early as possible and ensure

that they are aware that once they have accepted a place, pupils are expected to attend. It is often helpful to arrange a meeting for parents early on in the process, so that you can outline the pro-gramme of events and answer any questions that they might have.

- Plan the programme carefully; the aim is to provide challenge but to enrich the normal curriculum in a way that is engaging and fun. Some pupils may be reluctant to attend further schooling in their holidays – how will your programme encourage them? Offering activities that are not usually possible in school are often a motivating tool; similarly, changing the venue and the staffing to involve different personalities can be a successful way of making the summer school 'different'. Having a theme for the summer school and relating the names of the teams and the activities to the overall theme can also provide interest. Try to balance more academic activities with practical and problem-solving activities out of doors, that offer opportunities for leadership and team work.

- If possible use links with the local community, partnerships, governors, etc. to support the summer school. Having outside tuition is helpful in that 'experts' come in to work with the pupils who often see visitors as having more status and kudos. The knowledge of an expert can provide teaching in areas that you could not hope to cover by using your own teaching staff, and they may also act as role models for the pupils involved. In addition, the use of external tutors can reduce the pressure on your own teaching staff in the delivery of the programme.

♦ Build in time for evaluation and reflection. Generally the LEA will require you to give feedback on the achievements made by the pupils, so try to have a clear idea of how you will monitor and evaluate the success of the programme. It is also useful to provide feedback to the schools who recommended pupils and, where pupils are transferring to new schools, to forward information to them also.

The opportunity to attend summer schools can also be provided through other agencies. The National Academy provides a range of courses at universities throughout the country such as Durham, Exeter and Lancaster. Subjects include: Psychology, Law, The Economics of Sport and Leisure, The Mars Rover, and Cutting Edge Music Technology. Pupils need to be of secondary age and courses are residential and run for two weeks. Generally both the parents and the school/LEA are expected to contribute to the funding although in exceptional cases this might be waived.

Your local university may also offer activities in which able pupils can get involved, such as archae-ological digs. It is worth contacting them directly to find out what courses, if any, they offer. There are also a number of residential educational centres who offer weekend and more lengthy courses designed for able pupils.

Advanced Learning Centres

Advanced Learning Centres are coordinated by the National Primary Trust, and there are now more than sixty ALCs established across the country. They are set up within specific areas to provide children with opportunities to follow a challenging curriculum in particular subject areas, such as Mathematics, English or History. The teaching takes place after school or at weekends, and is often provided by local secondary teachers or by visiting experts. The National Primary Trust hopes that more centres will be created in different areas; further information about how to go about setting up an Advanced Learning Centre can be obtained from www.npt.org.uk.

Useful Resources

There are a variety of resources available to support provision for gifted and talented pupils. The list below is by no means definitive but may provide a starting point for reference.

Organizations:

The National Association for Able Children in Education (NACE)
PO Box 242, Arnolds Way, Oxford, OX2 9FR
www.nace.co.uk
NACE provide specialist advice and information to teachers and LEAs. They can provide training, conferences, speakers, support for particular projects as well as publishing a wide range of materials and

resources which can support gifted and talented delivery.

The National Academy for Gifted and Talented Youth (NAGTY)

www.warwick.ac.uk/gifted/

More detailed information on this organization is provided earlier in this chapter. The Academy, based at Warwick University, provides a wide range of support for teachers, pupil and parents. Online forums and residential summer schools can be accessed through them.

Brunel Able Children's Education Centre (BACE)

Tel: 020 8891 0121 Fax: 020 88918274

www.brunel.ac.uk/faculty/ed/

Based at Brunel University, this group specializes in providing support for those teaching gifted and talented pupils.

National Association for Gifted Children (NAGC)

Tel: 01908 673677 Fax: 01908 673679

Email: amazingchildren@nagcbritain.org.uk

www.nagcbritain.org.uk/

This is a site which is useful for both parents and teachers. It includes an interesting questionnaire 'Is My Child Gifted?' to complete online as well as details of how to become a member, online forums and various publications and other support for the gifted and talented.

Centre for Studies on Inclusive Education (CSIE)

Tel: 01179 238450 Fax: 01179 238460

http://inclusion.uwe.ac.uk/csie/csiehome.htm

Able, Gifted and Talented

A site concerned more broadly with inclusion for all pupils, but providing some interesting material on auditing how inclusive your school really is.

The Support Society for Children of Higher Intelligence (CHI)
Tel: 01386 881938
www.chi-charity.org.uk
A charitable group which provides information, offers membership and runs Saturday classes for able pupils.

The Sutton Trust Ltd
Tel: 02087 883223 Fax: 02087 883993
Email: sutton@suttontrust.com
www.suttontrust.com
The Sutton Trust aims to support projects that provide educational opportunities for young people. Pupils can obtain funding to support involvement in a variety of projects, particularly sixth formers attending summer schools at top universities.

Websites

The **DfES** standards website contains a wide range of information about provision for gifted and talented children. There are subject-specific lesson plans to build in challenge, and information on the use of mentors and enrichment activities. The website is managed by the Standards and Effectiveness Unit (SEU) of the DfES and provides online services for teachers to help raise standards of achievement in schools.
www.standards.dfes.gov.uk

Northumberland LEA has an excellent teaching and learning website with lively resources and links to other useful websites. It contains a variety of reports on gifted and talented activities in the LEA and information on auditing and policy writing.
www.northumberland.gov.uk/CS_Education.asp

Devon Curriculum Services offers useful information on identifying and monitoring able pupils, policy writing and enrichment activities.
www.devon.gov.uk/dcs/a/talent

Xcalibre provides subject specific resources for teachers of able pupils.
www.xcalibre.ac.uk

Aim Higher is a project designed to challenge post-16 pupils who are gifted and talented.
www.dfes.gov.uk/aimhigher

The DfES Standards/KS3 Strategy website – The National Strategy for Key Stage 3 offers a good opportunity for thinking about how to offer suitable programmes of work for gifted and talented pupils. Like other pupils, they are entitled to opportunities, support and challenge that will help them to reach their potential.
www.standards.dfes.gov.uk/keystage3

The **QCA website** has sections on 'Identifying gifted and talented pupils', 'School and subject policies', 'Roles and responsibilities', 'Managing Provision', 'Matching teaching to pupils' needs' and 'Transfer and transition'.
www.nc.uk.net/gt/

The World Class Tests website – World Class Arena is a global initiative designed to identify and nurture gifted and talented students around the world. The website consists of tests, resources and support materials. It is a global forum for sharing and comparing results worldwide and will continue to grow and evolve as the project expands.
www.worldclassarena.org

Books

Curriculum Provision for the Gifted and Talented in the Secondary School by Deborah Eyre and Hilary Lowe (David Fulton Publishers 2002). This book provides a useful introductory section with a school-wide overview followed by subject-specific chapters. There is a companion book, *Curriculum Provision for the Gifted and Talented in the Primary School* (2001) edited by Deborah Eyre and Lynne McClure.

Listening to Able Underachievers: Creating Opportunities for Change by Michael Pomerantz and Kathryn Anne Pomerantz (David Fulton Publishers 2002). Aims at raising attainment in secondary schools, with specific reference to those who underachieve. The book is based on extensive research and interviews with pupils and teachers.

Teaching the Very Able Child: Developing a Policy and Adopting Strategies for Provision by Belle Wallace (David Fulton Publishers 2000). This is a useful starting point for drawing up a whole-school policy and thinking about how to tackle provision for the able pupil in a mainstream school.

Useful Information and Resources

Teaching Mathematically Able Children by Roy Kennard (David Fulton Publishers). A subject-specific guide for providing challenge and developing those who are gifted in Mathematics.

Effective Resources for Able and Talented Children by Barry Teare (Network Educational Press Ltd). A photocopiable resource file designed to meet the needs of gifted and talented pupils in the primary and secondary sectors. Subjects covered include, Humanities, Literacy, Mathematics and Science.

Effective Provision for Able and Talented Children by Barry Teare (Network Educational Press). This book looks at provision for the able pupil in all respects across the school, including advice on creating policies, pastoral issues and practical enrichment activities.

Thinking Through Primary Teaching by Steve Higgins, Viv Baumfield and David Leat (Chris Kington Publishing 2001). A resource file which provides a range of material designed to engage pupils and encourage them to talk about thinking and learning. Different strategies are provided to cover a wide range of subject areas.

Also in the same series *Thinking Through Geography*, *Thinking Through History*, *Thinking Through Religious Education* and *Thinking Through Science*.

Effective Learning Activities by Chris Dickinson (Network Educational Press 1996). Practical ideas combined with theory, suggests methods to improve the teaching and learning outcomes in the classroom.

Able, Gifted and Talented

Closing the Learning Gap and *Strategies for Closing the Learning Gap* by Mike Hughes (Network Educational Press). The first provides the theory of how improvements to teaching and classroom practice can improve learning; the second provides more practical resources and approaches.

Accelerated Learning in the Classroom by Alistair Smith (Network Educational Press 1996). How to make greater use of the brain, multiple intelligences and strategies to raise pupil motivation and achievement.

Developing Students' Multiple Intelligences by Kristen Nicholson Nelson (Scholastic). Practical ideas to integrate into lessons; aimed more at primary students than secondary.

The Challenge Award. Provision for Able, Gifted and Talented Pupils: A Self-Evaluation Framework for Schools and LEAs (a NACE Publication 2003). This is a folder that provides schools with a framework for what to do in practice to raise standards for able, gifted and talented pupils; what to look for as evidence of impact on learning; and how to become skilled in school self-evaluation. It may be used as a planning tool, an audit tool or for assessment, and can usefully lead to a whole-school action plan for improving provision for able, gifted and talented pupils. This publication focuses on provision at all levels and for all ages from nursery to post-16.

Gifted and Talented Children With Special Educational Needs: Double Exceptionality by Diane Montgomery (a NACE/Fulton publication 2003). This book focuses on the issue of gifted children with special educational needs, whose giftedness is often overlooked in the classroom. It is a practical text that gives advice about how to make provision for these pupils within the mainstream school.

Periodicals

The Gifted and Talented Update provides news items and details of research relating to gifted and talented pupils and lists relevant training courses that are on offer. It is specifically designed for Gifted and Talented Coordinators and is a useful way of keeping up-to-date with developments. **The Gifted and Talented Update** is published by Optimus Publishing, who may be contacted by phoning 020 72519034; or find further details on their website at www.optimuspub.co.uk.

Aspire is the house magazine of the National Academy for Gifted and Talented Youth. It provides news about the Academy, details of courses and summer schools, as well as publishing contributions from pupil members of the Academy.

Contact The National Academy for Gifted and Talented Youth, The University of Warwick, Coventry, CV4 7AL or www.warwick.ac.uk/gifted/

National Research Publications

Providing for gifted and talented pupils: An evaluation of Excellence in Cities and other grant-funded programmes, OFSTED, 2001.

Able, Gifted and Talented

www.ofsted.gov.uk/public/docs01/giftedand
talented.pdf

Highly Able Children: Third Report from the Education and Employment Committee 1998–1999, London, HMSO: 1999.
www.parliament.thestationery-office.co.uk/pa/
cm199899/cmselect/cmeduemp/22/2202.htm

Educating the Very Able: Current International Research, Joan Freeman, Ofsted, 1998.
www.archive.officialdocuments.co.uk/document/
ofsted/veryable/able.htm

Grant-Funded National Programmes

Independent/state school partnerships

The scheme was set up in November 1997 and has since supported 120 partnerships in around 400 schools involving about 36,000 pupils. The aim of the scheme is to strengthen links between the maintained and independent sectors through drawing on mutual expertise and resources (not all programmes cater for gifted and talented pupils).
www.dfes.gov.uk/indstatepartner/summary.shtml.

Excellence in Cities: the gifted and talented strand

Excellence in Cities (EiC) began in 1999 as a major initiative involving 24 LEAs in six major conurbations. It has now been extended to a further 31 LEAs and 12 clusters within LEAs and covers primary schools and the post-16 sector. Its structure is based on partnerships between LEAs and schools. EiC has a number of strands, one of which is 'gifted and talented'. The strand is based on the conviction that high achievement is possible for some pupils in all schools.

www.standards.dfes.gov.uk/excellence/policies/GiftedAndTalented/

Appendix 1

Draft Policy For Gifted and Talented Pupils

Rationale

The school seeks to provide a secure and challenging environment that stimulates the development of all pupils, ensuring that no 'ceiling' is put on achievement. The school recognizes that there are pupils who have a very high general ability across the curriculum (gifted) or who have a talent in a specific area. These pupils must be identified, challenged and supported in order to ensure that their individual needs are met both within, and outside, the curriculum.

Aims

The school aims to:

◆ provide stimulating learning experiences for all pupils that encourage independence and autonomy, and support pupils in using their initiative;

◆ provide opportunities for pupils to work at higher cognitive levels;

◆ provide opportunities for pupils to develop specific skills and talents;

◆ encourage pupils to reflect on the process of their own learning and to understand the factors that help them to make progress;

◆ foster the development of a well-rounded and balanced individual, both intellectually and socially;

♦ encourage pupils to be open to ideas and initiatives presented by others, thus promoting the importance of citizenship and collaboration.

Definition
Gifted children will be identified as those who are performing significantly above the expected level in a number of different curriculum areas. They will show a combination of some of the following characteristics:

♦ facility with language use;

♦ logical reasoning ability;

♦ imagination and creativity;

♦ ability to link concepts and ideas;

♦ ability to question ideas and concepts;

♦ wide reading;

♦ wide general knowledge;

♦ excellent memory skills;

♦ humour;

♦ ability to engage in problem solving;

♦ interpersonal skills;

♦ intrapersonal skills;

♦ bodily/kinaesthetic skills;

♦ rapid assimilation of material;

♦ focused concentration on specific tasks;

♦ musical ability;

♦ keen observation.

♦ The specifically talented will show a range of these characteristics in a particular subject area.

Appendix 1

The school will identify pupils who have the potential to be gifted and talented and are underachieving in all or some curriculum areas. The school will seek to find strategies to meet the individual needs of these pupils.

Identification

The school uses a range of agreed criteria and sources of evidence. These may include:

- NFER tests;
- information provided at all points of transition, both external (for example, primary to secondary) and internal;
- Standard Assessment Tests, including SATs;
- World Class Tests;
- reading tests;
- CATs tests;
- MidYIS;
- YELLIS;
- Alis and ALPS;
- in-school monitoring system;
- subject-specific criteria for identifying the most able;
- staff recommendations;
- information from parents, carers and other outside agencies.

The school keeps records of those pupils who show particular or overall high ability within the curriculum. It is recognized that pupils develop at different rates, therefore the number and members of the identified group of pupils will change over time. Staff should actively use all available information to inform planning and pupil progression.

Provision
School level

- setting by ability within subject areas when applicable;

- differentiation and extension within individual teacher's planning, to provide challenge for gifted and talented pupils within the curriculum;

- withdrawal for specific activities that allow gifted and talented pupils the opportunity to work together on challenging and enriching tasks;

- involvement of gifted and talented pupils in extra-curricular activities that extend the boundaries of the curriculum.

Within the classroom the learning culture should:

- be pupil centred, valuing and utilizing pupils' own interests and learning styles;

- encourage the use of a variety of resources, ideas, methods and tasks;

- encourage metacognition, or 'thinking about thinking';

- provide a secure learning environment where risk taking is valued;

- provide a challenging learning environment, allowing pupils to access the higher-order thinking skills;

- involve pupils in working in a range of settings and combinations: as individuals; in pairs; in groups; as a class; cross-year; cross-school; and inter-school;

- encourage pupils to ask questions of themselves, of their peers, of adults, and of ideas;

- encourage target setting that involves pupils in their own learning and progress;

- celebrate creative and original thinking;

- ensure that homework extends the learning of the individual pupil, encouraging independence and self-motivation.

Outside the classroom the school will actively seek:

- opportunities for able, gifted and talented pupils to take part in enrichment activities outside school, for example: Challenge Days; Masterclasses; mentoring younger pupils; peripatetic music teaching; sporting events; dramatic productions; competitions; residential courses;

- collaboration with outside agencies that provide guidance, ideas and support for able, gifted and talented pupils, for example: NACE; NAGC; National Academy for Gifted and Talented Youth;

- involvement of adults (parents, local businesses, universities) with abilities and knowledge in specific areas, in order to motivate and inspire able, gifted and talented pupils;

- opportunities for able, gifted and talented pupils to participate in Gifted and Talented Summer Schools.

Coordination, monitoring and review
There is a named whole-school coordinator with specific responsibility for identifying and monitoring the able, gifted and talented pupils in the school. The coordinator works closely with the Leadership Team, with the staff, and liaises with parents. Monitoring is closely linked with progress reviews and the annual reports to parents. Records of identified able, gifted and talented pupils are regularly reviewed through monitoring data and teacher recommendations.

Appendix 1

Resources

- staff Inset time;
- staff and department meetings;
- centralized whole-school resources, including useful web addresses;
- LEA Gifted and Talented Network Meetings and Inset;
- outside agencies; for example NACE, NAGC and The National Academy for Gifted and Talented Youth at Warwick University;
- publications, for example *Educating Able Children* (NACE); *Teaching Thinking* (Questions Publishing); the *Gifted and Talented Update*;
- Centre for Able Children at Oxford Brookes University;
- AST time.

Appendix 2

Example Parent Questionnaire

This questionnaire has been designed to provide more information about pupils in this school who have been identified as able, gifted or talented. It will not be used for assessment purposes. We should be grateful if you would complete the form, providing the relevant detail in order for us to ascertain the best ways to support and develop your child.

Name of child:

Year/Form: **Age:**

Which of the following do you feel is the best description of your child? (Please tick)

☐ Has general intellectual ability; appears to be highly able in a number of areas with well developed vocabulary, memory and reasoning.

☐ Has specific talents or ability in one particular area, e.g. Mathematics, Sport or Drama. Please identify which area in particular: ....

....

☐ Has leadership potential; demonstrates the ability to lead and guide groups of people, cooperates well with others and demonstrates confidence in this respect.

☐ Has highly developed practical skills; appears to be physically able to manipulate objects, displays spatial awareness and mechanical/engineering skills.

☐ Is a creative and unusual thinker; comes up with unusual ideas, challenging questions and inventive solutions to problems.

In terms of thinking and reasoning, which of the following do you believe applies to your child? (Please tick any comments that you feel are appropriate.)

☐ My child displays a strong ability to reason and deduct.

☐ My child is able to summarize/generalize, drawing together strands of information from a wide range of sources.

☐ My child is able to see relationships, even between objects/arguments that appear to be unrelated.

☐ My child is able to grasp and solve problems quickly and efficiently.

When studying or encountering a new subject my child:

☐ Displays intellectual curiosity and pursues an interest in a persistent manner.

☐ Asks numerous questions which may be searching in nature, and challenge the responses given.

☐ Appears to learn more quickly than others.

☐ Is quickly able to memorize and recall new information.

I would describe my child as (please tick any/all that are appropriate):

☐ An avid and wide ranging reader.

☐ A reader who displays an interest in books/magazines/newspapers which are normally considered to be suitable for older children or adults.

☐ Displaying a wide vocabulary in speech and/or writing. He/she is accurate in language use and makes use of complex sentence structures. He/she enjoys words and word games.

☐ Someone who is easily able to understand mathematical concepts, who likes to play games related to numbers and/or manipulates numbers accurately.

☐ Displaying the ability to talk/read/write early (please delete any that do not apply).

☐ Having a strong creative ability, demonstrated through an interest in music, dance, art or drama (please specify). He/she may react with sensitivity to music and/or rhythm.

Do you feel that your child has particular ability in any of the following areas (please tick):

☐ Sporting/athletic ability.

☐ Artistic/creative ability.

☐ Social skills – the ability to communicate with, engage and involve others.

☐ Musical ability.

☐ Leadership skills.

☐ Ingenuity – coming up with creative or inventive solutions to problems.

☐ Reading or study skills.

☐ Other – please provide details . . . .

My child:

☐ Communicates well with others.

☐ Tends to prefer the company of older children or adults.

☐ Is comfortable with his/her peer group.

☐ Tends to prefer his/her own company and to work alone.

☐ Will spend more time and energy than his/her peers on a topic that is of particular interest.

☐ Asks questions and has an enquiring mind.

☐ Sets high personal goals.

☐ Tends to find innovative ways of approaching a problem or a topic.

☐ Is self-sufficient.

☐ Has a 'quirky' sense of humour.

What particular hobbies or interests does your child have outside of school? (Please list)

Which extra-curricular activities does your child choose to participate in at school? (Please include any additional music tuition received through school.)

What organizations does you child belong to? For example, Brownies/Cubs/Scouts/Guides Cadets, volunteer groups, sporting clubs, etc. (Please list)

Please give any other information about your child that you feel may be helpful to the school.

Bibliography

Black, P. and Wiliam, D. (1998) *Inside the Black Box: Raising Standards Through Classroom Assessment*, Kings College London.

Bloom, B. S. (ed.) (1956) *Taxonomy of Educational Objectives: Book 1 Cognitive Domain*, New York: David McKay Company, Inc.)

Eyre, D. and Lowe, H. (eds) (2002) *Curriculum Provision for the Gifted and Talented in the Secondary School*, London: NACE/Fulton.

Eyre, D. and McClure L. (ed.) (2001) *Curriculum Provision for the Gifted and Talented in the Primary School*, London: NACE/Fulton.

Hampshire County Council (1998) *Challenging Able Pupils: Guidelines for Secondary Schools.*

Ofsted (2001) 'Providing for Gifted and Talented Pupils', Ofsted Publications.

Pomerantz, M. and Pomerantz, K. (2002) *Listening to Able Underachievers*, London: David Fulton.

DfES (2004) *Excellence and Enjoyment: Learning and Teaching in the Primary Years*, DfES Publications.